TRADITIONAL USUI REIKI
LEVEL I, II, MASTER MANUAL

Lisa Powers

Copyright © 2018 by Lisa Powers

All rights reserved. This book or any portion thereof may not be reproduced or used in any manner whatsoever without the express written permission of the publisher except for the use of brief quotations in a book review.

Printed in the United States of America

First Printing, 2016

ISBN-13: 978-1537683775

ISBN-10: 1537683772

https://onlinereikicourse.com

https://lisapowers.co

Thank you for purchasing this book, please visit

https://onlinereikicourse.com/manualgift for a special gift.

Note from the Author

Please keep in mind that the information and techniques in this book do not constitute medical advice. Seeking medical advice from a qualified doctor in the case of serious illness is always recommended. The information is this manual is provided with the highest intentions however, the author cannot accept responsibility for any illness that occurs as a result of the reader not seeking medical advice from a qualified doctor.

This manual will provide you with a clear and detailed guide through Usui Reiki Levels I, II and Master. At the end of this course, you will have the knowledge you need to begin performing reiki on yourself, other and using it as a tool for your own personal growth. You will also have the ability to perform attunements with your students. Please note that you must receive the Reiki attunements associated with each level. Attunements will be discussed later on, but are an integral part of becoming an effective Reiki practitioner.

To remain true to the original content taught by Mikao Usui, information outside of the scope of Traditional Usui Reiki will be identified. Much of this manual will focus on the original **Usui Shiki Reiki Ryoho healing** modality formalized by Usui.

This information is for educational purposes only and is not intended to replace the advice of your doctor or health care provider. I encourage you to discuss with your doctor any questions or concerns you may have regarding any imbalances or conditions you are experiencing.

As a thank you for walking on this Reiki path with me, you can download a special free gift from me, as well as receive exclusive course discounts at https://onlinereikicourse.com/manualgift

Table of Contents

Note from the Author 3
Introduction to Energy 1
Things to Do to Enhance Your Energy 3
Reiki Energy 5
    Entrainment 6
    How Does the Body Use Reiki Energy? 8
    Chakras 9
The History of Reiki 15
    The Legend of Dr. Mikao Usui 15
    The History of Usui 16
    Chujiro Hayashi 19
    Hawayo Takata 20
Reiki Branches and Associations 23
The Reiki Principles 27
    Just for Today I Will Not Worry 29
    Just for Today I Will Not Be Angry 29
    Just for Today I Will Do My Work Honestly 30
    Just for Today I Will Give Thanks for My Many Blessings 31
    Just for Today I Will Be Kind to My Neighbour and Every Living Thing. 32
Working with Reiki 33
    The Attunement Process 33
    During The Attunement Ceremony 35
    After the Attunement Ceremony 37
    A Healing Crisis 40
    Meditation for After Your Attunement 43
Reiki Applications 45
    Animals 45
    Plants and Vegetation 46
    Food and Drink 47
    Additional Uses for Reiki 47

Anatomy for Reiki 49
The Muscular System 51
The Endocrine System 52
Organs 53
The Lymphatic System 54

Working with Reiki - Self 57
Benefits of Daily Self-Treatments 59
How to Perform Self-Treatments 60
Self-Treatment Hand Positions 61
Performing Reiki on Yourself Consistently 62

Performing Reiki with Others 65
Where You Perform Reiki 65
Preparing for a Session 67
Setting your Intention 68
Working with the Aura 69
Considerations When Working with Others 69
Prescribing and Diagnosing 72
Beginning The Reiki Session 74
Full Body Hand Positions 76
Closing the Session 76
Time Constraints 77

Group Reiki Sessions 79

Reiki and Pregnancy, Babies & Children 81

Reiki and Palliative Care 83

Conclusion 85

Level I Review 89

Reiki Level II 91

Applications for Reiki Level II 93
Reiki Symbols 93

Cho Ku Rei – The Power Symbol 95
How to draw the Cho-Ku-Rei 96
How to Use the Symbols 97
Ways you can use the Cho Ku Rei (CKR) symbol 98

Sei He Ki – The Emotional Healing Symbol 99
How to draw the Sei-He Ki 100

Hon Sha Ze Sho Nen – The Distance Symbol 103
- How to Draw the Hon-Sha-Ze-Sho-Nen Symbol 105
- How to Use the Hon-Sha-Ze-Sho-Nen Symbol 107
- How to Draw the Reiki Symbols..109

Gassho 111

Reiji-Ho 113

Chiryo 115
- Summary...116
- Breath..116
- The Dan Tian 117

Distance Reiki...119
- Ways to Perform Distance Reiki..120
- The Surrogate Method..121
- Using your body as a Surrogate...123
- Visualizing during Distance Reiki 124
- Creating Your Mental Reiki Room 124

How to Perform a Distance Reiki Session 129
- Permission..129
- Steps to Performing a Distance Reiki Session 131

Distance Reiki Possibilities 133
- Performing Reiki Across Time..133
- Performing Reiki with the Future 134
- Performing Reiki with the Past..134
- Past Lives and Reiki..135
- Transcending Time and Space in Self-Treatments...............136
- Reiki in the World...137
- Working with Groups 138

Using Reiki with Your Goals 139
- Problem-Solving with Reiki 141
- Preparing To Work with Clients 143
- Using Tools..144
- Working with the Aura 145

Starting Your Reiki Practice 147

Non Traditional Reiki Symbols 151
- Reverse Cho Ku Rei 152
- Harth 153
- Johre 154
- Midas Star 155
- Motor Zanon 156
- Raku 157
- Zonar 158

Combining Reiki with other Health Modalities 159
- Working with Your Past, Present and Future 160
- When a Client Does Not Feel Reiki 160

Animal Reiki Techniques 163
- Communicating with Animals 164
- Preparing to Perform an Animal Reiki Session 164

Reiki Level II Conclusion 167

Master Level Introduction 171

Reiki and Symbology 173

The Traditional Usui Reiki Master Symbol 177
- The Reiki Master Symbol 178
- How to draw the DKM (Traditional) 179
- Where You Can Use the DKM in a Session 180
- Using the Dai Ko Myo 181
- Variations of the DKM 182

Non Traditional Usui Reiki Master Symbols 183
- Two Versions of the Dumo or the Tibetan Master Symbol 183

The Reiki Attunement Ceremony 187
- The Hui Yin and the Violet Breath 188
- The Hui Yin 189
- The Violet Breath 189

Non-Traditional Reiki Attunements 191

Preparing for the Reiki Attunement Ceremony 195
- Master Preparation 196

How to Perform Reiki Attunements 199

Performing Each Attunement Separately 211
Level I First Attunement 211
Level I Second & Third Attunements 212
Level I Fourth Attunement 213
Level II Attunement 215
Master Level Attunement 216

Distance Reiki Attunements 219
Benefits of Performing Reiki Distance Attunements 220
Preparing to Perform Distance Attunements 220
Mental Reiki Room 220
Surrogate 221
Using Information to Connect During a Distance Attunement 221
Steps to Performing the Distance Attunement 221
How the Recipient Should Prepare for the Attunement 222
Student Experiences during the Attunement Ceremony 223

Advanced Reiki Techniques 227
Psychic Surgery 227
Visualization 228
The Technique 229

Accessing Different Levels of Consciousness 231
Using Reiki in Spaces 234
Reiju Meditation for Self 236
Performing Reiju with Others 237
Distance Reiju 239
Living Reiki 239

About the Author 243

Introduction to Energy

All things are infused with energy. As a species, we have been fascinated by this energy and the power it has within our own bodies as well as the world around us. This energy that permeates our bodies goes by many names such as chi or consciousness.

At the point of conception, this energy infuses our bodies and is the intelligence that helps each cell to divide and find purpose to become the trillions of cells that make up our amazing body. Science has confirmed the presence of this energy and using tools such as Kirlian photography, developed in the late 1930's can capture visual proof.

With this understanding, practices have been developed to help develop and balance this personal energy. Reiki, Qigong, Tai Chi, Meditation, Yoga, and Feng Shui are just a few of the many ways individuals can enhance the flow of this energy.

We are all born with the power to heal ourselves. Our bodies are in a constant state of maintaining balance. It is that energy within that helps the body to repair and replace aspects of itself as needed.

In the distant past, our ancestors had an innate wisdom that they used to heal themselves and maintain vitality. Over time, with our focus shifting to what is outside of ourselves, we have lost the ability to clearly see within.

In comparison to our own personal energy, Reiki is the energy that connects our higher self with everything around us. We can use Reiki energy to help us balance our own energy and bodies.

We are in a time where science is beginning to validate the existence of the energies that surround and exist within each of us.

The Buddhist proverb: When a student is ready, the teacher appears is often true in the case of Reiki. You may have found this course at just the perfect time in your life. Reiki is the intelligent life force that connects us to what we need.

Things to Do to Enhance Your Energy

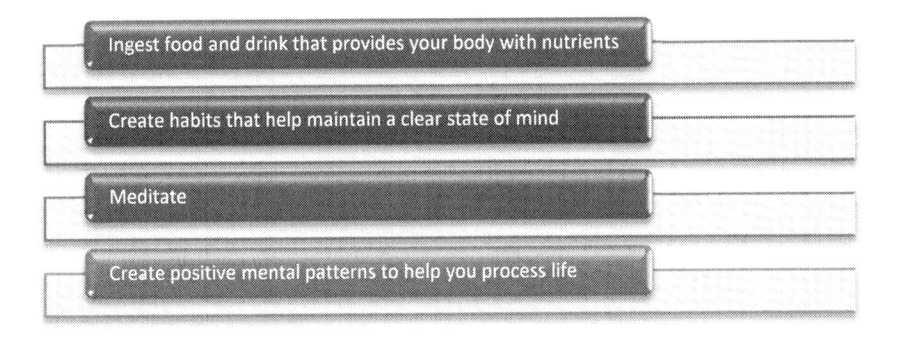

- Ingest food and drink that provides your body with nutrients
- Create habits that help maintain a clear state of mind
- Meditate
- Create positive mental patterns to help you process life

Our potential is tremendous but in order to become the powerful beings we were meant to be, we need to change our focus. Reiki is not only a tool for physical healing, but mental and spiritual growth as well. When Dr. Usui first formalized Reiki, he intended it to be a tool for spiritual growth. The physical healing that occurred was a side-effect of the increased awareness.

Reiki is a gift that is given to each and every one of us. By opening your mind to this energy, you will be more capable of seeing the synchronicity in your life and be able to let your life flow. You already have access to this amazing life force. This course will show you how to use it.

We intuitively use Reiki energy. When we were children and were hurt, we were soothed by our Mother's caring touch. A symbolic kiss to make it better actually did ease the pain as Mother and child used Reiki energy to soothe and heal. We naturally hold and protect areas that we have injured and in doing so are also drawing in Reiki energy to those parts to help them recover.

This energy is plentiful and is available to everyone. There is no single person or organization who holds the rights to this energy. Reiki is not trademarked or patented. The only thing you need to access Reiki energy is the intention to align yourself to it and then the willingness to surrender your intellect so your heart can lead the way.

Reiki Energy

Although Reiki has traditionally been used as a healing system, it is also extremely effective as a way to help individuals increase awareness, insight, wisdom and personal growth.

Our bodies are energetic in nature. Our bones resonate at lower frequencies while our blood, thoughts etc. vibrate at higher frequencies. This magnetic pulse is known as a bio magnetic field. In Eastern traditions this pulse is also known as Ki or Prana. It is interesting to note that scientists have found that measuring the magnetic fields of the body with magneto cardiograms and magneto encephalograms often provide a more accurate indication of what is happening in the body than traditional electrical measurements.

When a practitioner is performing a healing session, the energy that emanates from their hands produce a significantly larger bio magnetic reading (7-10Hz – Theta and Alpha range) than a non-practitioner. These frequencies are associated with physical healing.

Contentment, relaxation, decreased feelings of stress, fear and anxiety as well as a reduction and in some cases elimination of physical illnesses and persistent conditions are common observations from clients after a Reiki session. There are countless case studies and anecdotal research verifying the effects of Reiki sessions.

Entrainment

Entrainment is the tendency for two oscillating bodies to lock into phase so that they vibrate in harmony. In 1665, Dutch Physicist and Scientist Christian Huygens found that when he placed two clocks with pendulums on a wall close to each other and swung the pendulums at different rates, eventually they would end up swinging in sync at the exact same rate. Huygens realized that this concept applied to not just pendulum clocks, but as a basic law of physics.

During a Reiki session, the practitioner places their hands on or just above a client's body. The practitioner conducts universal energy from their arms, and out through their hands where it flows into the client's body. When a practitioner and client come together they are the two oscillating/vibrating objects discussed in the definition of entrainment. Every cell in our body and every atom in the universe is in a constant state of vibration. The tendency for two objects is to lock into phase so that they vibrate in harmony. In most cases, the weaker of the two oscillating objects will have a tendency to adjust to the stronger vibration which is Reiki energy.

In a Reiki session the practitioner does not rely on their own personal energy, rather they are conduits for focusing the energy from the world around them. We are born with the innate intelligence of Reiki and it illuminates our bodymind, stimulating balance and growth. Over time however, habits and beliefs that do not serve our highest good can stifle that flow of energy resulting in a loss of vitality and eventually imbalance.

What sets Reiki apart from other forms of touch therapy are the attunements that the practitioner receives. These attunements open the channels in an individual so they are in direct contact with universal life force. After an attunement, these channels are open forever. In Reiki Level I, four attunements are given. Reiki Levels II and III have one attunement each.

Reiki does not create new abilities in a practitioner, instead it reveals abilities that they already had. Like plugging a lamp into in an outlet that already has electricity, Reiki helps the practitioner make the connection. Like turning on the lamp, all the practitioner needs to do to activate the energy is to place their hands on themselves or others or visualize doing so.

Although there are many modalities that have been developed to stimulate the flow of energy within a bodymind, in comparison Reiki is easy to learn and practice. It is also a modality that benefits the practitioner as well as the recipient and can be used as an extremely effective tool for personal growth as well as healing on all levels.

Reiki Level I focuses on the health of the practitioner. After this level, individuals can perform Reiki sessions on themselves as well as others who are physically present. It can take three to four weeks to adjust the initial attunements. Individuals may find shifts occur in their dreams, energy levels or experience minor detoxification symptoms. The practitioner will feel well as they shift through the changes that occur as a result of more energy entering their aura and chakras. At times of discomfort, the practitioner may find that performing a Reiki session either on themselves or others will help to balance the energy. It is recommended that especially in the first month after an attunement that the Reiki practitioner performs Reiki sessions on themselves and others daily.

In a Reiki session, the energy drawn in by the recipient is done so through the practitioner's hands. The energy will go where it is needed and in the order that the recipient's bodymind determines. If you have never had the benefit of receiving a Reiki session, you need to schedule a session with a practitioner you feel called to work with. You must experience a session in order to fully understand it.

Reiki is available to everyone at any time. However, the Reiki attunement aligns the bodymind in a way that increases the flow of this energy significantly. Measurements of the energy emitted from an attuned practitioner's hands versus a non-attuned practitioner illustrate the importance of the attunements.

Like a wireless connection, we know the signal is present even if we cannot see it. When we make a call on our cell phone or use our computer with a Wi-Fi hotspot, we are tuning into that frequency which results in us connecting with other people and information. Reiki energy is a life force like that signal except that we are the towers and satellites that are the conduits which harness this energy from all around us.

An attunement helps ensure you have a clear connection with the energy and continued Reiki sessions ensure your reception remains strong. An attunement is an alignment that will be with you for the rest of your life. Like programming a specific number into your phone, you will always have Reiki on speed dial.

How Does the Body Use Reiki Energy?

We understand that every particle vibrates at a specific frequency. That frequency in more esoteric terms can be termed consciousness. This consciousness is what activates all parts of our body and synchronizes the events within our body.

Each day, our body is working to maintain balance. When we consider exercising, our body begins its preparations well before we begin our workout. When cells are separated from our body, even the thought of cutting oneself ignites a series of reactions in those extracted cells because it is the same frequency that animates them and the body.

Our body has a natural electromagnetic frequency that it prefers to resonate with. When all levels of the body are in harmony with that frequency, communication is strong. The body loses its effectiveness to heal and maintain homeostasis when the lines of communication within the body are disrupted. These disruptions occur when we store energy that is dissonant with our natural resonance.

We tend to store energy in the form of memories and beliefs and as they accumulate around the same theme, the strong dissonance begins. Where our body once operated as a perfectly timed symphony, with conflicting energy stored, we have many instruments out of tune and sync.

When a body receives Reiki energy, it is like having a light to make the body aware of the energy that is not serving it. The practitioner does not decide what needs to be released or when, the wisdom of the body does. The practitioner holds the space for the bodymind to see the possibilities it can choose from with regard to healing so the body is no longer tied to a dysfunctional way of being.

Once the body has chosen what it is ready to address, it can systematically release the stored energy at a cellular level connected with the imbalance. The cells then begin functioning as intended and the healing occurs on a physical as well as emotional, mental and physical level.

The body does not need to be consciously aware of what beliefs and memories it is working with which is one reason why Reiki can be so effective. Many of our strongly help beliefs were developed in early childhood or even fetal life.

The client just needs to ensure that as the releases occur that they are aware of the process and allow them to fall away.

With the body vibrating at a more natural state, harmony and peace on all levels can be restored.

Chakras

Chakra means spinning wheel of energy or energy centre in Sanskrit. Each of these centres is associated with specific organs, endocrines, issues, emotions, colors and elements. Balancing these centres can have a physical, emotional and spiritual effect on an individual.

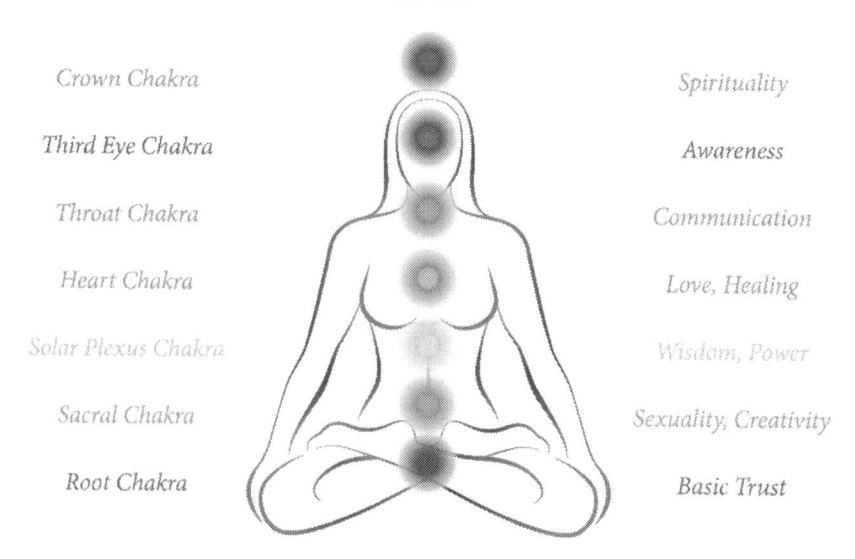

Crown Chakra	Spirituality
Third Eye Chakra	Awareness
Throat Chakra	Communication
Heart Chakra	Love, Healing
Solar Plexus Chakra	Wisdom, Power
Sacral Chakra	Sexuality, Creativity
Root Chakra	Basic Trust

It is not only important that each individual chakra be balanced, but that they also be balanced in relationship to each other. The lower three chakras are considered masculine in nature and call us to action. They help to ground us and are usually concerned with the material world. The higher three chakras are feminine in nature and are associated with self-reflection and the spiritual aspects of life. The heart chakra is balanced in masculine and feminine energy and can help to balance other chakras.

Chakra	Location, associated organs and endocrine glands, emotion	Imbalanced expression	Balanced expression
Crown	Close to top of brain, pineal gland, bliss	Limited connection with Divine or Source, limited access to body's inner wisdom, mental imbalances.	Experiencing Source and Source within self, wisdom, awareness, self-realization.

Third-eye 	Between eyebrows (within head), Pituitary gland, fear and imagination	Focused on physical plane, poor vision, close minded, headaches, sleep issues, mental and hormonal issues.	Healthy intuition, creative, ability to manifest, strong memory and balanced hormones.
Throat 	Throat area near larynx, thyroid, vocal chords, expression	Speaking from programmed conditioning, overly talkative or non-communicative, thyroid issues, metabolic and hormonal conditions, coughing.	Strong communicator, expresses personal truth, maintenance of healthy weight.
Heart 	Heart center (behind physical heart), heart, lungs, thymus gland, love and joy	Not accepting love, problems in relationships, holding grudges, heart issues, lung issues and immune system imbalances.	Ability to love and receive love, healthy immune system, balance in relationships and other chakras, compassion, feelings of harmony and peace.
Solar plexus 	Along spine in upper abdomen, liver, gall bladder, pancreas, spleen, stomach, anger, sense of purpose	Unsure of role on earth, feelings of rejection, extreme extroversion or introversion, ulcers and issues with organs associated.	Healthy digestion of food and life. Feeling a sense of personal power, confident

Sacral	Behind and a little below the navel, feminine aspects of kidneys, reproductive organs, joy and desire	Imbalances around sexuality and creativity. Possessiveness and jealousy, immune system issues, low self-esteem	High self-esteem, healthy expressions of creativity and sexuality, joy and pleasure.
Root	Base of spine, kidneys, adrenal glands, fear and passion	Insecure, resistant to physical world, spaced out, fatigue, fear around survival	Feeling grounded, motivated and comfortable in this material plane.

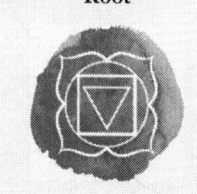

As you can see, an individual with physical imbalances in a specific area may also reflect the imbalanced qualities associated with the connecting chakra.

In a Reiki session you will not only be balancing physical aspects of the recipient's body, but also their energetic centers. By balancing these centers, the physical body will also be addressed.

In a session with another practitioner, you may have been told that specific chakras were blocked. Keep in mind that you are the best judge of your body and when a practitioner diagnoses, they are doing so through their own filters.

When you work with clients you will likely get a sense over time of how the energy is flowing through the body. Keep in mind that in some cases, underactive or over active chakras may be doing their work to assist with an imbalance in another area. By assuming that the chakras are the issue, you would be trying to "fix" a coping strategy the body is using until the root cause is healed. This is why we do not diagnose, keep an open mind and allow the body to choose what is healed and in what order.

At certain times we will all display symptoms of one or more chakras being out of balance. This usually means there are beliefs, energy or emotions tied to the concepts associated with that chakra that are not serving you. Reiki self-treatments as well as being open to seeing things in a new light can help you start to release that storage that may be impacting the chakra.

The History of Reiki

When word of mouth is used to pass on traditions and historical information, it tends to be adapted. Although Mikao Usui is credited as the founder of Reiki, it is widely thought that this form of healing has been around for centuries and that Usui rediscovered this art in the late 1800's. The account below is the story that has been passed down from Master to student. This story is now thought to have been adapted to appeal to western culture. A more detailed account follows this excerpt.

The Legend of Dr. Mikao Usui

Growing up in a family with strong beliefs in Zen Buddhism, Mikao Usui developed a fascination with Western culture and later studied allopathic medicine. Usui became ill during a cholera epidemic in Tokyo. When struggling to live, Usui had a spiritual awakening which led him to join a Zen monastery.

According to legend, during his studies Usui discovered a method of healing that had been used for centuries. Included in this method were hand positions and symbols that could be used. Although Usui was eager to begin using this method, he felt he needed more awareness to effectively use it. He then focused his attention inward and began to develop his meditation practice.

As a part of his spiritual quest, Usui took a trip up Mt. Kurama. It is told that once he reached the top of the mountain, he picked up twenty-one stones, sat down and began his meditation. As each day passed, he threw away a pebble. He spent his time in meditation and study.

At the end of the 21 days, Usui set the intention that he was open to seeing things clearly. Legend has it that a bright light flashed above and rushed towards him, beaming through his forehead. Usui saw the symbols he was studying in the Sutras and is thought to have experienced enlightenment during this time. As Usui trekked down the mountain, he hurt his foot, and instinctively placed his hand on the injured area and observed the bleeding stop and the pain diminish.

During his travels, Usui stopped in a village. He ate a complete meal without discomfort despite the fact that he had been fasting for 21 days. Usui was able to heal the girl who served him food who was experiencing pain. Usui returned to the monastery and was able to heal his superior who was in pain with arthritis.

Usui decided to use Reiki with the homeless people in the poor areas of Kyoto. Usui spent time performing Reiki with the hopes of helping the beggars heal and become productive members of society, but was disheartened when he found them returning to their old methods of begging.

Usui was reminded that healing the body, spirit and mind as a whole is essential. Usui retreated to a period of meditation again. This is when Usui received the five principles of Reiki. The remainder of Usui's life was spent practicing and teaching Reiki.

The History of Usui

This information is what was passed down from Madam Takata (more information on Takata will follow). Anything that has been disproved through research has been excluded.

Mikao Usui Usui was born on 15th August, 1865 in Taniai-village, Yamagata- district, Cifu Prefecture. At a very early age, Usui entered a Tendai Buddhist school near Mt. Kurama. Usui was known for his gentle character and his honest and candid mannerisms. Usui enjoyed learning and reading and explored a variety of topics including medical science, religion, divination, history and psychology. Usui travelled to Europe, America and studied in China. Usui also studied kiko, the Japanese version of qigong. Usui noted that the healing techniques he was learning depleted the energy of the practitioner and he wondered if it was possible to heal without using the energy of the practitioner.

Eventually Usui became the secretary to Shinpei Goto, head of the department of health and welfare who later became the Mayor of Tokyo. Usui was also a member of the Rei Jyutu Ka, a group dedicated to developing psychic abilities. In March 1922, Usui was having difficulties in his business and personal life and enrolled in Isyu Guo, a twenty-one-day training course sponsored by the Tendai Buddhist Temple located near Mt. Kurama. Fasting, meditation, chanting, and prayers were a likely part of the practice. There is a small waterfall on Mt. Kurama where people stand under to meditate. This practice is believed to activate the crown chakra. Japanese Reiki Masters think that Usui may have used this meditation as part of his practice. It was during the Isyu Guo training that Reiki energy entered Usui's crown chakra. He became aware of his ability to use this life force to heal himself and others with immediate results.

Usui wanted to share this gift with others and moved to Aoyama Harajuku, Tokyo in April, 1922 and established a centre where Reiki was taught and given to the public. Usui called his system of healing Shin-Shin Kai-Zen Usui Reiki Ryo-Ho (The Usui Reiki Treatment Method for Improvement of Body and Mind) or in its simplified form Usui Reiki Ryoho (Usui Reiki Healing Method).

In 1923, the Kanto earthquake hit Tokyo with an estimated 140,000 people dying and the city in ruins. Usui performed Reiki on as many individuals he could and began training other Shihan (teachers). It was also at this time that he developed methods including a more formal Reiju (attunement) process.

The lowest degree of Usui's training was called Shoden (First Degree) and was divided into four levels: Loku-Tou, Go-Tou, Yon-Tou, and San-Tou. (Note that Mrs. Takata taught this level by combining all four levels into one.) The next degree was called Okuden (Inner Teaching) and had two levels: Okuden-Zen-ki (first part), and Okuden-Koe-ki (second part). The next degree was called Shinpiden (Mystery Teaching), which is what we now call Master Level. At the time, Usui used three symbols. He did not use a master symbol.

People lined up to receive Reiki and the time came when the centre could no longer accommodate the large numbers of people. Usui built a new center in Nakano just outside the city in 1925.

Usui travelled to share Reiki in places such as Kure, Hiroshima, Saga and Fukuyama. At an inn where Usui stayed while travelling, he suffered a stroke and passed away March 9th 1926. It is believed that his grave is at Saihoji Temple, in Suginami, Tokyo, although some claim that his ashes are located elsewhere After Usui died, his students erected a memorial stone next to his gravestone. Contrary to what has been told in the West, there is no "lineage bearer" or "Grand Master" of the organization started by Usui.

It is estimated that Usui taught over 2,000 students and initiated 20 teachers, some of whom continued to teach Reiki after Usui passed away. The twenty teachers initiated by Usui include Toshihiro Eguchi, Jusaburo Guida, Ilichi Taketomi, Toyoichi Wanami, Yoshiharu Watanabe, Keizo Ogawa, J. Ushida, and Chujiro Hayashi. The Japanese government issued Usui a Kun San for his honourable work.

Chujiro Hayashi

Chujiro Hayashi was a physician and retired Marine commander. Before he died, Usui asked Hayashi to open his own Reiki clinic and to expand and develop Reiki Ryoho based on his previous experience as a medical doctor in the Navy.

Hayashi opened a school and clinic called Hayashi Reiki Kenkyukai (Institute). After Usui passed away Hayashi left the Gakkai (Reiki society founded by Usui). At Hayashi's clinic, careful records were kept of all the illnesses and conditions that were addressed. He also made notes of which Reiki hand positions worked best to treat various ailments. Based on these records and notes, Hayashi wrote the Reiki Ryoho Shinshin (Guidelines for Reiki Healing Method). This guide was part of the class manual Hayashi gave to students.

Hayashi altered the way Reiki sessions were given. Rather than have the client seated in a chair and treated by one practitioner as Usui had done, Hayashi had the client lie on a treatment table and receive treatment from several practitioners at the same time. Hayashi also created a new system for giving Reiju (attunements). In addition, he developed a new method of teaching Reiki that he used when travelling. In this method, he taught both Shoden and Okuden (Reiki I&II) together in one five-day seminar. Each day included two to three hours of instruction and one Reiju (attunement).

Hayashi travelled to Hawaii in 1937 prior to the Japanese attack on Pearl Harbor, and was asked by the Japanese military to provide information about the location of warehouses and other military targets in Honolulu. He refused to do so and was declared a traitor. Hayashi performed seppuku (ritual suicide) in response to the disgrace that his family faced in light of his decision. Hayashi died on May 11, 1940.

Hawayo Takata

Mrs. Hawayo Takata brought Reiki from Japan to the West in 1937 and continued to practice and teach until she passed away in 1980.

This is a summary of Mrs. Hawayo Takata's version of her years leading up to her contact with Reiki at the Hayashi clinic. Takata stated that she was born on December 24th, 1900, on the island of Kauai, Hawaii. Her parents were Japanese immigrants and her father worked in the sugar cane fields. Takata married the bookkeeper (Saichi Takata) of the plantation where she was employed and they had two daughters. In October 1930 Saichi died at the age of 34. After five years of long hours of labor to support her family, Takata developed severe abdominal pain and a lung condition, and had a nervous breakdown. Soon after, one of Takata's sisters died and it was her responsibility to travel to Japan, where her parents had resettled to deliver the news. After informing her parents, Takata entered a hospital and stated that she was diagnosed with a tumor and gallstones, appendicitis and asthma. She was told to prepare for surgery but chose to visit Hayashi's clinic instead.

Mrs. Takata was unfamiliar with Reiki but was impressed that the diagnosis from the Reiki practitioners at the clinic closely matched the doctors at the hospital. She began receiving treatments. Takata wanted to learn Reiki in order to continue treating herself and also to take it back to Hawaii to share with others. Hayashi allowed Takata to work at his clinic and also began giving her Reiki training. Takata worked one year at the clinic and eventually received the Shinpiden level (Reiki Master). Hayashi officially acknowledged this in Hawaii on February 21, 1938, and also stated that she was one of thirteen Reiki Masters trained by him.

Takata practiced Reiki in Hawaii, opened several clinics, one of which was located in Hilo on the Big Island. She gave treatments and initiated students up to Reiki II. Takata became a renowned healer and travelled to the U.S. mainland and other parts of the world teaching and giving treatments. She attributed her success to the fact that she performed a lot of Reiki on each client. Takata would often do multiple treatments on a client, each sometimes lasting hours, and often initiated members of a client's family so they could give Reiki to the client as well.

Before Mrs. Takata died on December 11, 1980, she had initiated 22 Reiki Masters. These twenty-two Masters began teaching others with the promise to Takata that they would continue teaching Reiki in the same manner she had.

The exclusive nature of Reiki organizations in Japan made Reiki less accessible with individuals travelling to the US to learn it. Reiki practiced in Japan and in America is a blend of both western and Japanese Reiki. Takata is credited for helping Reiki flourish to the degree that it has in the western hemisphere.

It is estimated that there are over one million Reiki Masters in the world today with well over four million practitioners.

Reiki Branches and Associations

Many forms of Reiki have been developed to accommodate the various interests of practitioners and also as a way to trademark the modality so that students can only seek out instruction from specific instructors.

Please keep in mind that one branch of Reiki is no better than another. Each has a slightly different resonance depending on the Master who founded it and teaches it. Traditional Reiki holds the resonance of Dr. Usui but then is also flavoured by the lineage that follows Usui.

Although there are different branches of this modality, there is only one Reiki energy. No one has more or less access to it and it belongs to us all. As practitioners, we need to work together to promote Reiki. The different branches of Reiki are a reflection of the variations of the founder's energy at the time the branch was developed and not a different aspect of Reiki energy.

Together we can bring this gift of healing to the world. We need to embody the principles of Reiki and honor each other and the work we are doing.

There are several different associations throughout the world. If you plan on joining an association look at the benefits they will provide for the fees they charge. If they are advertising for you, look at how much traffic their website receives. What information will they provide you with? Will they require or charge you to use their certificates and manuals?

Although joining a Reiki association is not a requirement to start your practice as a professional Reiki practitioner, there are some benefits that an association can provide you with.

Because an association is an investment you will want to do your homework and ensure that the benefits an association provides you with equal or are greater than the cost to be a member.

Here are some things you will need to consider:

1. Is it important for you to be able to connect with other practitioners in your area and around the world?

    Most associations do not have closed discussion areas dedicated to members to share and connect around the topics that are important to them and their Reiki business. If this is important to you, make sure you choose an association with this option.

2. Are you wanting to demonstrate to your clients that you adhere to a code of conduct that demonstrates a high standard of professionalism?

    You will want to ensure the association you choose can provide you with a certificate of membership in either pdf form that you can print or one that is mailed to you. Please note that associations that mail your certificate may charge a significant amount more for that option.

3. Are you wanting to be able to access resources to help you build and manage a successful Reiki practice?

    Although most associations will have resources available for the general public on their website, they may not have detailed and comprehensive resources for you to use with regard to marketing and building your practice. You will want to see if there are additional resources available to members only.

4. Do you want some ideas around insurance companies that you can consider for your practice and liability insurance?

Fortunately, most associations will provide you with a list of companies you can explore for your insurance needs.

5. Are you looking for additional education that will help you as a Reiki Practitioner and your life?

Some associations will provide you with access to courses that you can take at a discount price to help continue your education.

6. Do you want help promoting your business to potential clients online?

Some associations will give you the option to post your practice and even courses on their website. This is one additional way you can gain exposure for your Reiki business.

7. Are you hoping to find ways to build your credibility as a Reiki expert?

You may wish to find an association that gives members the option to submit articles that can be posted on their website for potential clients. In some cases, you can include your contact information, so clients can contact you directly as well as establish you as an authority in your field.

These are some important considerations you will want to keep in mind when choosing an association. You will then want to weigh the cost of membership to see what is right for you. Most memberships charge a yearly fee while a few have a lifetime membership fee.

You need to do your research and then choose the organization that resonates with you and your Reiki practice.

In most cases with Reiki, clients will be attracted to you through word of mouth. Most individuals are not aware of associations so do not assume that you need to belong to one in order to be considered a credible practitioner. You can check with your municipal business license department to confirm that you do not have to belong to an association in order to practice Reiki professionally and then decide if an association will benefit you and your practice.

The Reiki Principles

Just for today I will not worry.
Just for today I will not be angry.
Just for today I will do my work honestly.
Just for today I will give thanks for my many blessings.
Just for today I will be kind to my neighbour
and every living thing.

The Reiki principles are a way to release the stories that your mind is telling you that create suffering as you go about your day. Most events in and of themselves are not stressful. It is the beliefs that we have about them that cause our stress. As you unravel and release those beliefs, you will find more balance and peace in your life. It is not possible to live every moment within these principles; however, you can continue to improve how you manage your thoughts and actions day to day, moment by moment. By focusing on these tenets, your conscious actions over time will become a natural way of being.

You may find reading the principles in the morning right when you wake up and evening before going to sleep helpful. You could also carry them with you or have them visible in a place you visit often or your healing room. The five principles will have a different resonance and meaning for each person and you may find that the feeling you have when you recite them now will be different than how you feel when you recite them tomorrow, next month and a year from now. You will need to commit time with them to see how they feel and what they mean for you.

With the focus of manifesting now being a popular practice, we tend to choose positive statements rather than negative so the traditional principles may not seem natural to you. If you need to reword the principles you can. In a positive frame they could be:

For all of today I will trust

For all of today, I will love

For all of today I will be true to myself and others

For all of today I will give thanks for my many blessings

For all of today I will be kind to my neighbour and every living thing.

You can also focus on the energy of each principle and what it feels like. Holding the intention is more important than the semantics of the principles.

When focusing on the principles, you may choose to be seated or lying down. You will close your eyes, repeating the ideals several times. You can try saying them out loud or in your mind and see what feels better at the time. Pay attention to the sensations you experience.

You may find it helpful to keep a journal with notes on your experiences that you can revisit so you can see how much things shift over time.

Just for Today I Will Not Worry

Worry is an emotion that although helpful in working through some situations, when in excess and occurring frequently, can be problematic, impacting the bodymind on all levels. This stress affects the circulation of energy within the body and impedes the inner wisdom that helps the body to regenerate.

Remember that when you are worrying, your mind is focused on the future. Although a small amount of worry can help you to take action in the present and plan for the future you desire, excessive worry can lead to confusion and stagnation. The only time you are effective is in the now. You need to trust that the wisdom of Reiki will guide you through all of life's ups and downs. The difficulties that we experience are usually a crucial part of our development.

If you develop a negative and fearful mind-set that causes you to worry, you will see even neutral events as negative. If, however, you release the beliefs that lead you to think of that situation as "bad" and be open to where it leads you, you can enjoy the ride that life gives you and be present for the ups and downs.

Make time each day for activities that bring you joy. It is also important that you are conscious of who you spend your time with. Seek out people who you resonate with that are peaceful and happy. Their energy is positively contagious.

Just for Today I Will Not Be Angry

Anger is usually a result of feeling a lack of power. When a negative event occurs and we have a strong belief we associate with that event, we may not process our emotions completely and our body will store the emotion. When a second event that reminds us of the first event occurs, our stored emotions emerge and we are then responding to both events with a heightened reaction. Over time, more and more emotions are stored until we become explosive when triggered.

It is a part of our work, to process those stored emotions. Anger is an emotion that can be difficult to process in a healthy manner because our society frowns upon its expression. When you are feeling anger, breath into it. Take a step back from the situation and become the witness of the event. From that view, you will be able to allow the emotion to pass rather than storing it.

On a daily basis, you can meditate on what the absence of anger feels like and choose to feel emotions that are higher in frequency. When feeling anger, take a deep breath, and then another until you feel the pressure of the anger release. The shift to a higher vibration will help your bodymind to transmute the stored anger.

Remember that every event and individual can teach us about ourselves and our perfection. When we come from that place of wanting to learn and being open, the lessons tend to be easier. When we respond to an event in anger, the lesson is not completed and we are destined to relive it with even more intense energy.

Just for Today I Will Do My Work Honestly

In your heart, you know when you are being honest. In your life, dissatisfaction can be your body's way of showing you that you are not being honest with yourself.

Leading a life where you are not honouring your dreams and talents is dishonest. Letting fear help you make your choices will guarantee that you are not being true to your heart and your soul.

Your role here on earth is extremely important. What you do and how you live does make a difference in the lives of countless people. Assuming otherwise is a falsehood that does not serve you or the world.

What is the impact you are here to make? The dreams you have are the desires that the universe wants for you. Make sure you are honouring yourself by following those dreams.

Just for Today I Will Give Thanks for My Many Blessings

Our ego tends to colour events as either good or bad. Our soul sees each event as an opportunity to strengthen and experience. Like steel is forged in fire and ice, our experiences take us to places we need to go in order to increase our awareness.

We spend much of our lives in the pursuit of things outside of ourselves in the hopes that they will make us feel good within only to realize that does not work. We think, I will be happy when....

Being grateful now will bring more things into your life that you can be grateful for. Work within and your environment will shift to meet the change in you.

Gratitude is an extremely powerful intention. It can not only raise the vibration of your bodymind but also bring insight and wisdom.

You have countless things to be grateful for. You need to focus on those things and that focus will bring much more into your life. Spending time while holding the intention of gratitude will have a dramatic effect on your life.

You may also choose to use Reiki to help you hold the focus of gratitude. Place one hand on the third eye chakra and the other hand at the base of the skull.

Just for Today I Will Be Kind to My Neighbour and Every Living Thing

Energetically, the frequency you emanate will attract more things of that frequency. If you hold a high vibration, you will bring people and things into your life with similar vibrations.

Dr. Masuro Emoto is known for his work with intention and water. In his research, he found that intentions that were negative in nature had a negative effect on water samples while positive intentions had a positive effect.

Our bodies are primarily water. Focusing on kindness and positivity will help ensure your bodymind is healthy. Individuals around us serve as mirrors. By being kind, the reflection you will see will also be positive. The choice to live a life of satisfaction and peace is yours. You are a powerful creator.

Remember that although Dr. Usui knew how to perform Reiki early on, it was his time spend in meditation and inner contemplation that helped him to increase his awareness so that he could be a strong conduit for Reiki energy. Please take time each day to meditate and perform self-treatments with the intent on releasing limiting beliefs you have about yourself and your world.

Working with Reiki

Because Reiki works on all levels, it can be used to help in countless ways. Individuals may seek it out to heal physical imbalances or find it when they are searching for answers to life's mysteries. Regardless of your history or reasons for pursuing Reiki, the way you will benefit the most from this modality is by being open to it. Fears and doubts will only create a veil of illusion that prevents you from having a clear view of what is possible. Take a leap and trust that you are learning this amazing art for a reason. Once you are attuned to Reiki energy, you will be able to connect with it whenever you choose for the rest of your life.

The Attunement Process

To effectively work with Reiki, you need to experience the Level I attunement ceremony, which consists of four attunements. Keep in mind that we are all already connected to Reiki energy but the attunement process helps your bodymind begin clearing dissonant personal energy so you are a clear channel to receive and be a conduit for Reiki.

Before receiving the Level I attunements there are some things you may wish to do to prepare. These guidelines are optional but will help enhance your experience of the course and the attunements.

Try to avoid alcohol or recreational drugs for two to three days before the ceremony. If habitual, these substances can serve as coping mechanisms that hide the beliefs that are causing suffering. When abstaining, our bodymind is alerted to the beliefs that are causing us to believe we have something to cope with in the first place and can then begin the work of dismantling those beliefs with Reiki energy. **Important: If you are consuming medication that is prescribed by your doctor, please continue to take the medication.**

If possible, the day before your ceremony try to eat and drink consciously. Have a day of whole foods including legumes, fresh fruit, and vegetables. Just as with alcohol and recreational drugs, we use food and drink to cope with stored energy and beliefs. By removing those crutches for a day, the stored energy, beliefs and memories that are not serving your highest self will become apparent for your body to begin healing.

Meditating each day for a week before receiving your attunements and ideally every day after can be very helpful. This will help you to become a clear conduit for Reiki energy.

If there is a period of time you will have to wait before your ceremony, having a daily meditation practice in place during that time will help you begin the shifts and you can then transition it to a daily Reiki self-treatment afterwards.

You can continue working through the course material as you feel called to. Some students choose to wait and sit with the information they have learned up to this point while other students decide to move forward. Follow what feels right for you.

During The Attunement Ceremony

During the attunement ceremony, the Reiki Master performs a routine that includes the Reiki symbols rediscovered by Dr. Usui. This ceremony is set for the highest good of the student and is intended to strengthen the connection between the student and Reiki energy.

A comparison would be just as you can program a radio station to specific channels or a phone number into your contact list, we can program ourselves to specific energetic frequencies. After the attunements, you have Reiki energy as a favorite and can access it whenever you wish.

Although you previously had access to Reiki energy, the attunement process ensures as the receiver you are clear and ready to receive the signal.

The attunement process generally takes 20-30 minutes. As the recipient, you just need to find a quiet space where you can relax. You may find playing some music or meditating during this time helpful.

During the time scheduled for your attunements, you may find you experience sensations or see images. You may find that you fall asleep. You may not notice anything at all. There is no correct experience and in each case, the ceremony is complete and successful.

I am often asked by students "I experienced this….is this normal?" As mentioned, some students see images, lights or memories while others feel sensations such as heat or cold or energy running through specific areas of the body. Others feel emotions rising while some students fall asleep. Some students do not have any sensations or images during the ceremony. Not experiencing sensations is not an indication of the shifts your body is processing on an energetic level.

Please remember that just as you are unique and there is no one else on this world like you, your experience with Reiki will also be special.

In my course, students have the choice to receive the attunements for each level at once or separately. As mentioned, Level I includes 4 attunements while Level II includes one attunement to the Reiki symbols and the Master Level includes one attunement to the Master symbol.

Essentially with each attunement, there is a release of dissonant energy which allows the recipient to return to a more natural frequency. After Level I, they are able to work with themselves, then with Level II they can work with others including the symbols and with the Master attunement can pass attunements on to others.

The second and Master level attunements help the student align with the symbols and the shifts usually occur as the student familiarizes themselves with the symbols, not solely during the attunement ceremony. Just as with Reiki sessions, during your attunements your body is choosing the amount of energy to draw in and what shifts it is ready to make. Nothing is being done to your bodymind, rather your bodymind is using Reiki as a light to see what aspects within are not serving your highest good. Your body then begins the work of shifting what it is ready to release. This is one reason why your self-treatments are so important after the attunements.

Personally, I find students are coming into the course ready to release and heal and return to their natural high frequency state. This is much more pronounced than even 5 years ago.

The idea behind waiting was a combination of the traditional approach of making sure a student truly wanted to embrace Reiki as well as helping them have a smooth and subtle transition as they begin working with Reiki.

On one hand I have seen dramatic shifts in an individual occur on all levels in an instant while at other times it has taken years and occurred gradually. Our minds are so powerful that if a Master tells a student, "you cannot handle more than one level of attunements at a time", most students will create that reality. Fortunately, we are moving into a new understanding where our previous limiting beliefs are being seen for what they are.

After the Attunement Ceremony

Some students find that after receiving their attunements, they can sense the energy flowing through their hands at different times. If you do not sense the energy right away that is completely okay. Remember that our body is only able perceive a fraction of the energy that surround us. It may time a little time for your body to refine its ability to perceive Reiki.

You may also find that your hands emanate energy when they are around people who need Reiki. This can feel like heat or cold in your hands and body. Over time you will get adjusted to the sensations and may find that the feelings shift over time and depending on who you are with. If you find your hands heating up and feeling uncomfortable, take a deep breath and set the intention that you allow Reiki to flow freely through you.

Your bodymind will also begin clearing and releasing of energy that is stagnant and no longer serving your highest good. The Reiki attunement has a powerful healing influence on the mind body and spirit, activating all seven chakras, beginning with the root, and ending at the crown chakra.

You may not feel any significant shifts right away. If you do start to feel some releases, surrender and know that your body is preparing you for healing and to be able to channel Reiki energy which is a higher level frequency. When you release the stored energy that is blocking the flow of energy through you, your body can be a clear conduit for healing. You may experience minor symptoms of physical cleansing and detoxification. Although some people call this a healing crisis, it is different because in this case, your body is choosing what to balance and shift. Nothing outside of you is forcing change.

If you are noticing changes, it is your body releasing dissonant energy including stored beliefs and memories that no longer serve you. Listen to your body. Rest when you need to, go outside and breathe when you can.

It is also very important that you perform a daily self-treatment on yourself. Place your hands on your body and allow Reiki to infuse your body with energy and allow it to process any stored energy, beliefs and memories smoothly and easily. You will also want to meditate daily.

The consumption of adequate amounts of water will also help this process flow smoothly. Some students note that they develop a headache, and ensuring you are hydrated can assist with this.

Reiki energy works on all levels of the mind, body and spirit. By surrendering and acknowledging that you are ready to heal and release stored emotions, memories and beliefs, you can be open to seeing your life in a new way and healing yourself. Trust your bodymind and do not resist.

Trust that Reiki and your bodymind will release what is not serving you so you can more clearly follow your purpose and lead a life filled with peace, love and joy. If you find emotions rising, be present with them. In most cases, just watching the emotions and not jumping into the story they are attached to is enough for them to rise and release. Do not analyze or try to assess the process-that is your ego's way of trying to stay in charge.

By accepting emotions as they arise as a part of your personal healing process and not attaching a great deal of importance to them, they will soon pass. After your ceremony, you may also find yourself dealing with certain issues in your dreams. That is your mind's way of processing the memories and beliefs. Although there are many ways to interpret dreams, remember that they are a part of you and your subconscious so you are the best person to discern their meaning.

If a dream is lingering, you may wish to meditate with the intention of taking any wisdom the dream provided while releasing the energy associated with the dream. Otherwise, once you have woken up you can release the dream unless you are guided to seek out further meaning. In some cases, actively trying to analyse a dream can undo the work your subconscious was doing around releasing some unnecessary information.

The attunements align you to Reiki energy. Using Reiki energy is a skill you will develop. Although you have access to it, your ability to be a conduit for it will grow with practice. After your ceremony, you will want to perform a self-treatment each day, ideally twice a day. We are in an ideal state of mind, first thing in the morning and before sleep at night so performing self-treatments then can have the most profound effect.

When you feel ready, you can begin to perform Reiki with others, but ensure you keep up your daily self-treatments.

A very important concept to understand is that **Reiki is not sent or directed, it is always drawn in by the recipient through the practitioner**. This is what separates Reiki and other types of energy work. The practitioner does not effort to manipulate the energy or decide where the energy should go. They are witnesses who observe the energy. Because the practitioner focuses on BEING rather than DOING, the practitioner is not using their own personal energy and will leave the session feeling energized from the Reiki that was drawn through them.

This is also why unlike other energy modalities; Reiki practitioners do not feel the condition of the recipient they are working with. The energy flow and information exchange is one way.

Practitioners who have learned other modalities that encourage the practitioner to direct and use their energy may find that by initially keeping their Reiki sessions separate from their other modalities will ensure that it is Reiki energy that is being used. They will then get a feel for the differences in the resonance of Reiki energy in comparison to the other energy they have worked with in the past.

With continued work with Reiki energy, you will likely find that your connection with your intuition is strengthened. As you release energy that does not resonate with you, you will connect with your energetic signature and the connection you share with everything and everyone around you.

A Healing Crisis

Our bodies are miraculous machines. Multitudes of amazing processes are occurring in you right now without you even needing to consider them.

Let's look at how inflammation occurs in the body.

At first, one incident occurs that causes stress in the body and triggers a defensive response. This could be a food that does not agree with you or a belief that causes you suffering.

Over time, if that substance continues to be ingested or that belief continues to trigger emotions your bodies defense stance becomes chronic and a new way of functioning.

If before we were operating at a level 7 on most days regarding mood and energy levels, with this chronic inflammation we now function at a level 5 and with more time that number continues to drop. We then regard this sub-optimal existence as the way it is.

Enter change.

Your friend recommends a new book, vitamin, course, therapist or modality to try and you decide to give it a shot.

Initially you don't feel too much and assume that "it didn't work". Then you notice you don't feel great. Now you assume that the new book, vitamin, course, therapist or modality has made you feel worse.

What is going on?

Sometimes learning or exploring something new causes us to take a step back and shift our perspective.

Imagine a big pot of minestrone soup. Just sitting there, it looks like a pot of broth with a smooth surface. Add some heat to it (new book, vitamin, course, therapist or modality) and all of the goodies that were always there under the surface now rise to the top.

So, did the heat create the vegetables and bits turning the soup around and creating ripples on what was a smooth surface? No – they were already there but the heat brought them to the surface. Just as the modality, therapist, course, vitamin or book did not cause the symptoms you are experiencing.

How does that help me feel better?

This understanding will ensure you take a conscious look at how you are feeling rather than attributing it to an outside factor and show you the power you have to heal what has been brought to your awareness.

Once you deeply acknowledge that the shifts you are experiencing are bits of yourself that no longer serve you, you can surrender to the feelings and sensations so that they can be transmuted into the wisdom you need to learn.

We have a tendency to resist discomfort or to try to push it outside of ourselves or deep within. These tendencies are what cause the inflammation (emotional, energetic and physical) in the first place. If you are feeling discomfort, breathe and sit with it. It has a message for you.

We can get into the technical labels such as Herxheimer Reaction, but the bottom line is that your body on a cellular level is releasing what does not serve your highest good. When your body needs to physically eliminate – whether it is going to the bathroom or vomiting, we do not hesitate and allow the process to occur. We understand that this process is natural and necessary. We need to extend this understanding and acceptance to energetic releases as well.

So what can I do?

Be gentle with yourself. This means that if you need to rest, rest. If you need to be around those you love and who bring you joy – do so. If you need to be alone, honor that.

Meditate. The energy that your body is choosing to highlight and release needs to be processed by you consciously. The belief that is not serving you needs to be neutralized. The emotions you have been storing need to be acknowledged and transmuted. Meditation will help you be present during this time to ensure you heal.

Stay hydrated. Water helps your cells function. This includes helping them release the storage they have that are impairing their function. Everyone is different with regard to the amount of water they need to be healthy so listen to your body's cues.

Breathe. We process our emotions through our diaphragm and when energy comes up to be released, we need to make sure we are consciously breathing.

Surrender. Try to trust and surrender to the release of the symptoms you are experiencing. Remember that this is your body healing itself.

Self-treatments. Perform Reiki on yourself every day. Try to see this time with yourself as a way to treat yourself with love. Allow Reiki energy to help you process the changes.

So – how are some ways you can tell this is healing or the worsening of a condition? First, you may feel better than you have in a while. Then, during the healing crisis/event, you do not have any negative emotions about the symptoms you are experiencing or identify with them, knowing that they are a part of your health improving.

Please keep in mind that these symptoms usually do not last for more than a few days and are usually fairly mild. If your symptoms continue or are worrisome, they are not connected to your energetic shifts and you should seek medical care.

Trust yourself and your body.

The information provided in this excerpt is for educational purposes only and is not designed to diagnose, prescribe or in any way replace supervision by a qualified physician. Please see your physician with any serious health concerns.

Meditation for After Your Attunement

You can perform this meditation for the 21 days following your attunement.

Find a comfortable position in a space that is quiet and free from distraction. You may wish to play some relaxing music and light a candle if you normally do so. For a few minutes, focus on your breath. Pay attention to how your body feels as you fill your lungs and release your breath. Envision a ball of light above you. The colour is your choice and should help you feel calm and relaxed. Imagine the light growing bigger and bigger until it fills the room. Breathe the light in and out feeling it bring in positive energy and release energy that no longer serves you. Now imagine you are in standing beside a waterfall of light. Step under the waterfall and allow it to wash your energy body clean. Stay there until you feel light and in a space of love.

This meditation can be done any time you feel the need.

Reiki Applications

Reiki energy exists in everything. Reiki can be used to help balance anything you choose. Use your imagination and see how Reiki can help you in your life. Here are some common things that Reiki can be used on.

Animals

Animals are sensitive to energy and tend to enjoy receiving Reiki. You can begin your Animal Reiki practice by performing Reiki with animals you know and when confident and ready you can move onto other animals.

Smaller animals can be held in your hands while you beam Reiki to them while with larger animals you can start at the front of their bodies and work your way back. Be sure to not make contact with animals that may bite or attack. In those cases, you can perform a distance Reiki session which you will learn in Level II.

Just as when working with humans, Reiki will go where it is needed in the order that is best for the recipient. One difference with animals is that they may guide you to the place that requires balancing by moving around until your hands are touching the place that needs to be addressed.

An Animal Reiki session does not have a standard set of hand positions or duration. Animals will let you know when the session is complete by resuming activity after a period of relaxation or by moving away. If you think working with animals will be the focus of your practice, you will want to receive some education about safe handling practices to ensure you create a safe environment for both the animal and yourself during your sessions. Being an Animal Reiki Practitioner can be extremely rewarding.

Plants and Vegetation

Reiki can be used to balance any form of vegetation in your environment. Because the energy of plants and trees extends far beyond their physical presence, it is vital that they are healthy so that their energetic influence is a positive one in your home and surroundings.

Experiments have been performed where seeds that receive Reiki each day grow more quickly than seeds that do not. Reiki can be given to plants by holding your hands 1-2 inches away from the plant. Trees can be balanced with Reiki by touching their trunks. You can also perform Reiki on the water being used for your plants and trees. You can use distance healing (Level II) to work on larger groups of vegetation such as gardens and forests.

Food and Drink

You can balance what you eat and drink. This will help ensure that your body receives the nutrients it needs from the substance while releasing anything that will not serve it. You can balance your food and drink by placing your hands above it and setting the intention that it will serve your body's highest good. You can also place your hands on your stomach after eating with the intention of a smooth digestion process.

Additional Uses for Reiki

Reiki has many uses and is not limited to people and animals. Because Reiki enhances your focus and energy you can use that increased awareness on anything you wish to have such as increased positive energy, clarity or resolution about. For example, Reiki can be used on your:

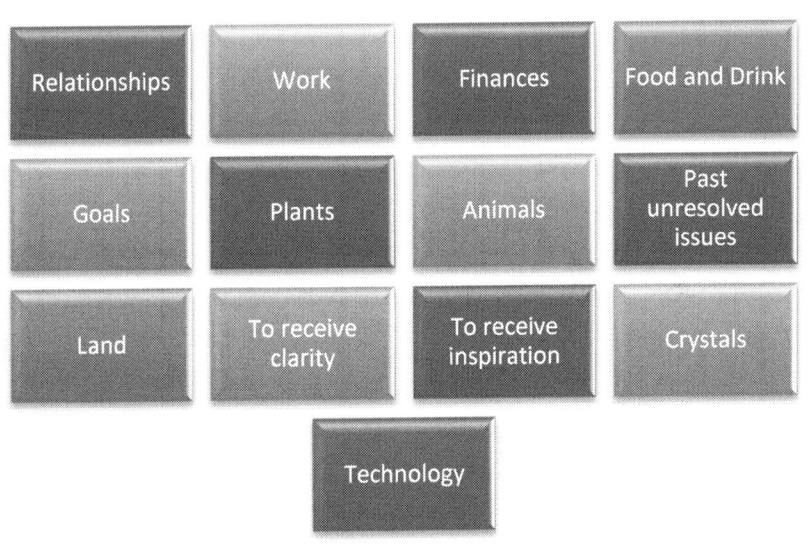

Relationships	Work	Finances	Food and Drink
Goals	Plants	Animals	Past unresolved issues
Land	To receive clarity	To receive inspiration	Crystals
	Technology		

There are so many other ways to use Reiki to help your life including (but not limited to):

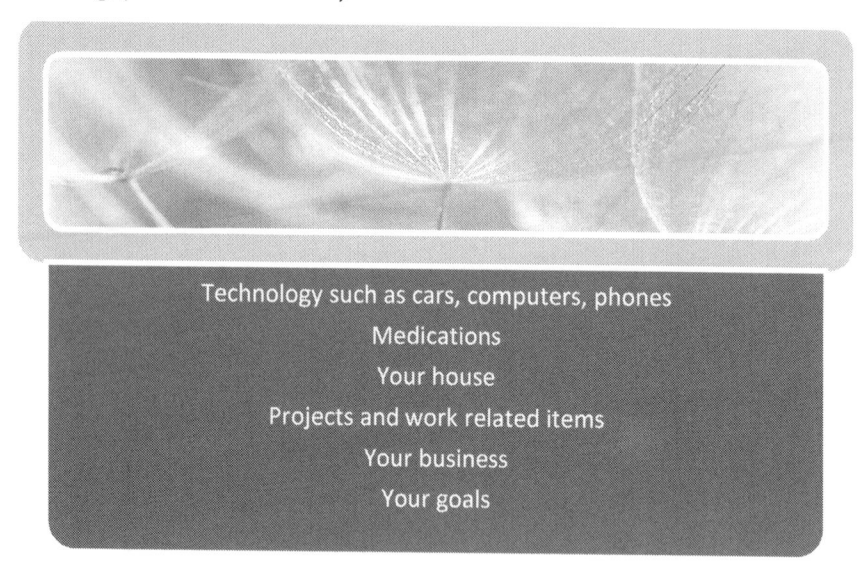

> Technology such as cars, computers, phones
> Medications
> Your house
> Projects and work related items
> Your business
> Your goals

Once you have been attuned to Reiki, the energy will flow through your hands whenever you touch with the intention of healing or helping.

Anatomy for Reiki

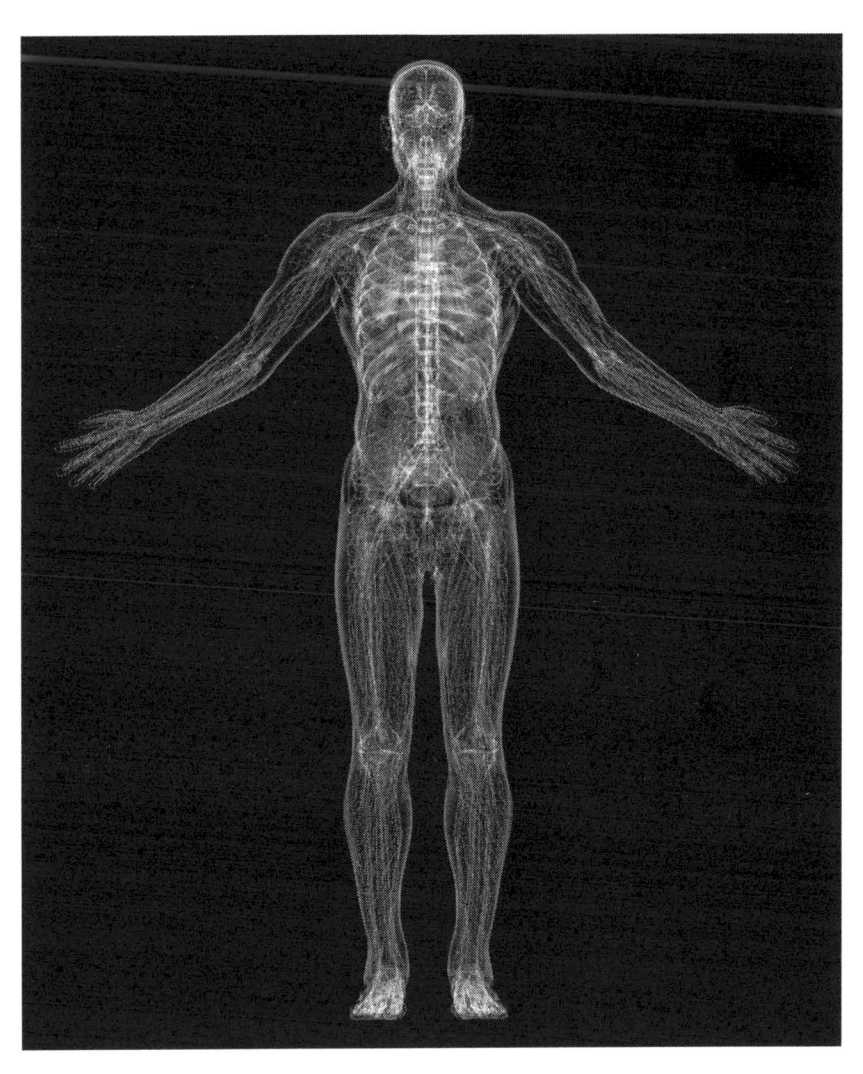

You have learned that your body uses Reiki energy and chooses what aspect requires balance and healing. Because the practitioner is not using a standard system of information and is instead allowing the inner wisdom of the body to choose what to balance and when, Reiki is extremely simple to administer. Having a basic understanding of anatomy and physiology will help you to be consciously aware of the conditions clients are coming to you with, but know that the knowledge will not impact your ability to perform effective Reiki sessions. During a session, all you need to do is place your hands above or on the recipient and allow the energy to be drawn through you. Although an individual may come to you with pain in a certain area, the source of the imbalance may be located in a completely different area or may not be physical in nature.

The following illustrations are diagrams of the human anatomy that you may find helpful in your visualization when working with others. If you decide to further your studies, there are many resources and courses available for free online.

The Muscular System

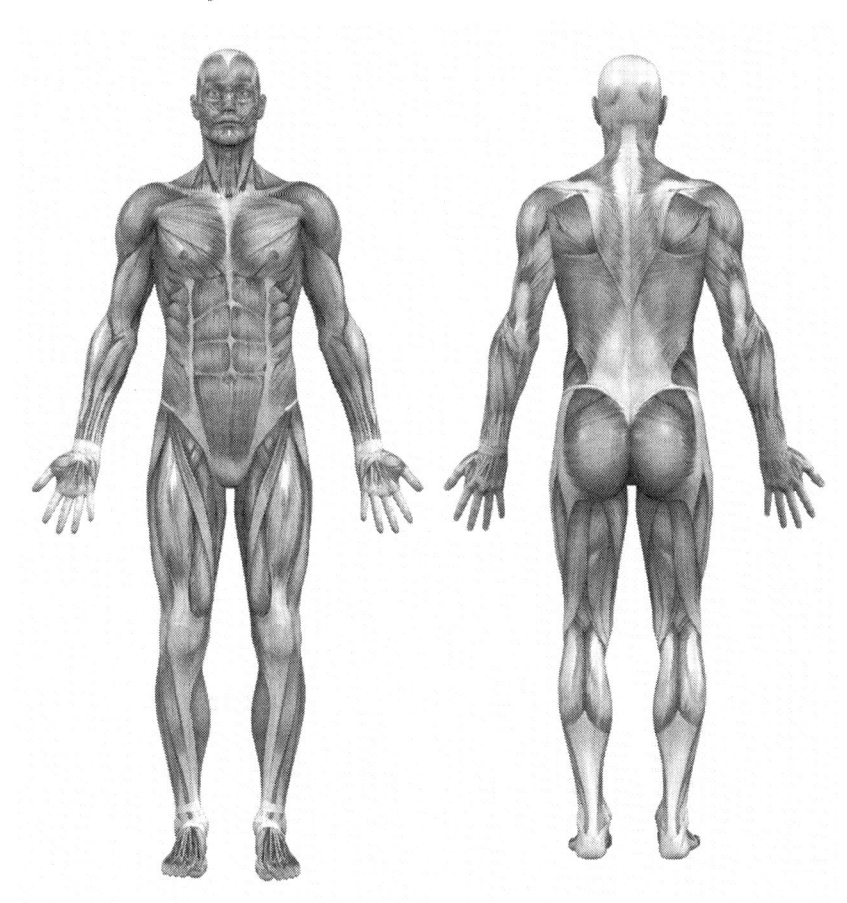

The Endocrine System

The endocrine system consists of glands that produce and secrete hormones that are chemical substances produced in the body which regulate the activity of cells or organs. These hormones regulate the body's growth, metabolism, and sexual development and function.

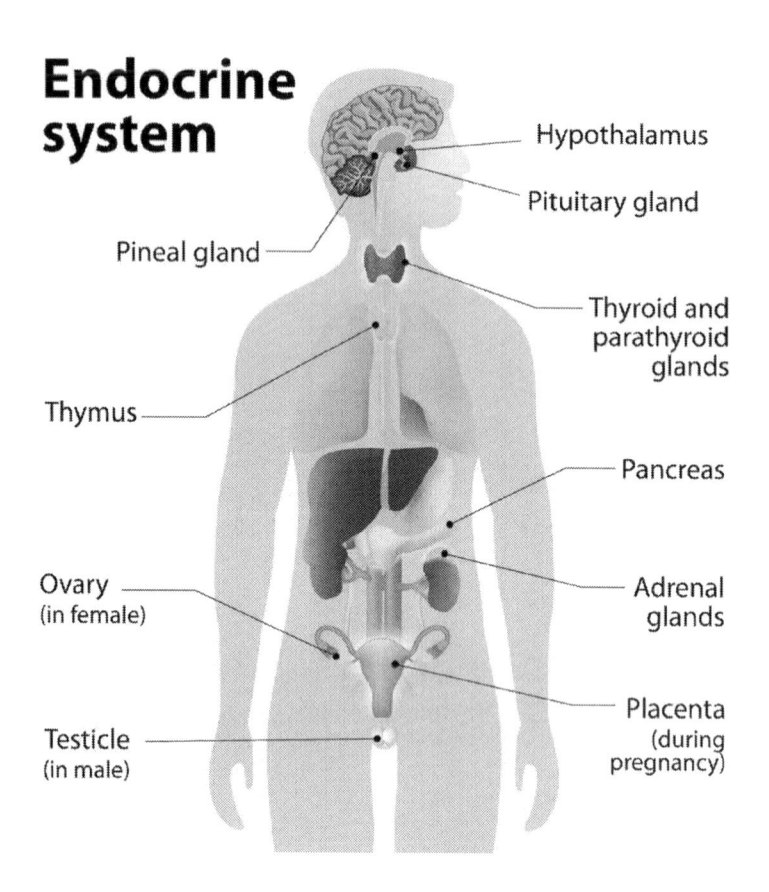

Endocrine system

- Hypothalamus
- Pituitary gland
- Pineal gland
- Thyroid and parathyroid glands
- Thymus
- Pancreas
- Ovary (in female)
- Adrenal glands
- Testicle (in male)
- Placenta (during pregnancy)

Organs

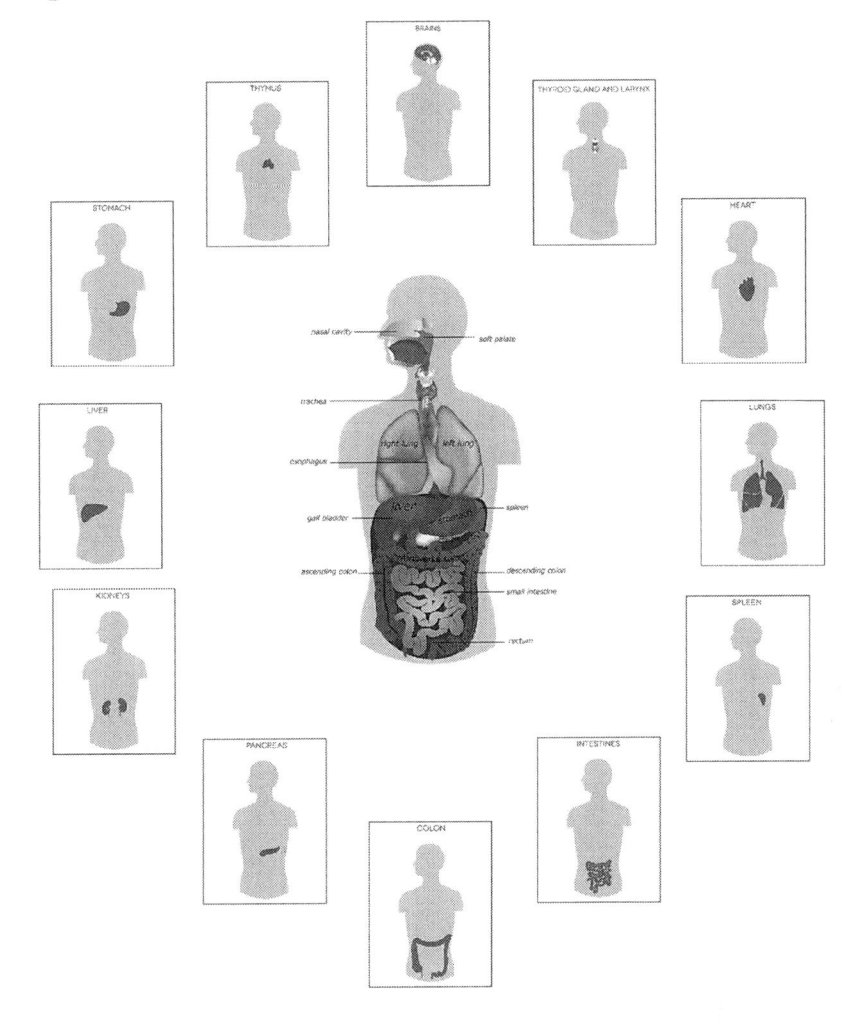

The Lymphatic System

The lymphatic system is a part of the circulatory and immune system and consists of thin vessels that run throughout the body and circulate a fluid called lymph. Lymph originates from the interstitial fluid that seeps out from the capillaries and bathes the cells. Lymph is a slightly yellow fluid that contains white blood cells, called lymphocytes, along with proteins and fats. After the fluid bathes the body tissues, it is stored in the lymphatic capillaries to flow back into the bloodstream via lymphatic vessels that reconnect with the veins close to the heart.

During that process, lymph is forced through the lymph nodes where germ fighting cells from the immune system reside. The nodes act as stations where the body addresses any viral or bacterial presence to prevent the imbalance from circulating through the rest of the body. Lymph nodes are small oval structures that are spread throughout the body and are located in clusters close to larger lymphatic vessels in the neck, chest, armpits, elbows, abdomen, groin, knees and ankles.

The lymph nodes play a role not only in our immune system, but are also areas where the production and storage of some of the body's lymphocytes and monocytes occur.

The spleen, an organ in the abdomen that lies under the left side of the ribs is an important part of our lymphatic system. Rather than filtering lymph, the spleen filters blood and plays a role in maintaining blood volume, production of some blood cells, recovery of debris from aging blood cells and the storage of blood platelets. Although in western allopathic medicine the spleen is not considered vital to the health of an individual (the liver can take over some of the spleen's activities if it is removed), from a Traditional Chinese Medicine perspective, the spleen is extremely important in influencing the cyclical activities of the body including the movement of fluid.

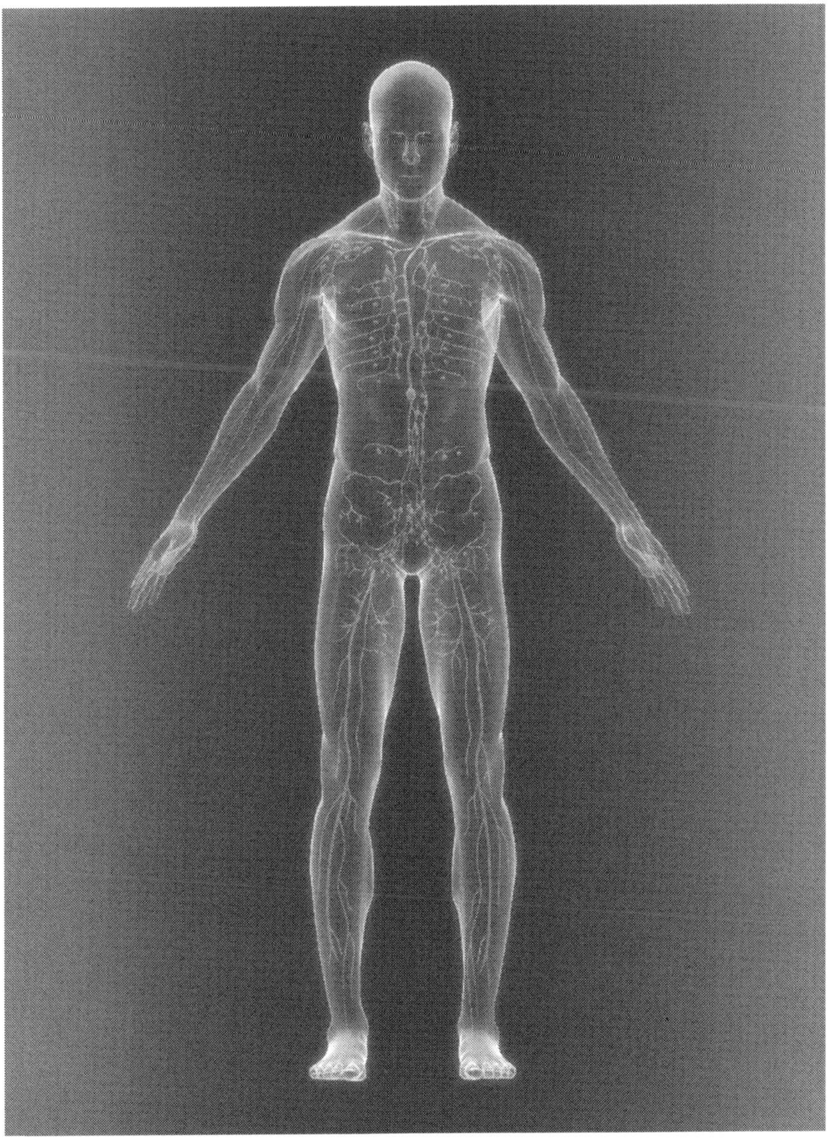

Working with Reiki - Self

Although you have always had a connection to Reiki energy, once you have received your attunements and have a basic understanding of what Reiki energy is, you are ready to work with the universal life force. Remember that with every profession you need to practice the skills associated with Reiki and even once you feel you have mastered them, continue to be open to learning. You will want to focus first on yourself, then work with people you feel comfortable with and then when confident and ready, expand your Reiki circle.

In time, with practice and experience you will be able to confidently call yourself a Reiki Master and feel completely in tune with Reiki energy and the skills and techniques you will learn here.

Please be gentle with your expectations around how your Reiki sessions should look and feel. Every session will feel different. It is natural that you will feel unsure and question yourself and even Reiki energy. Allow those fears to arise and see what they are connected to. Are there beliefs that are limiting you that you are ready to surrender?

Trust that as you continue your Reiki practice, your body will use the energy to help you gain increased clarity and balance.

I have encountered some Masters who do not perform Reiki on themselves and instead focus on others. Although they may be effective practitioners in a session, outside of the healing room their vibrations are low and they do not live the principles of Reiki. By working with yourself, you can get to a point where just by being yourself, standing in a line at a grocery store or performing mundane tasks at work, you are Reiki. Everything around you will benefit from your presence. In that state, real change in your environment will occur as your energy brings light to everything around you. Reiki can bring personal transformation on all levels. Perceived obstacles and setbacks are a natural part of the cycles of life, but with Reiki you will have the strength and awareness to deal with them. Even if you focus solely on yourself in your Reiki practice, balance and peace will be your reward.

We are taught that we must work hard at things in order to become proficient. We are also taught that anything worth having is worth working for. These beliefs can set us up for difficulty. Although it can take time to unravel the illusions we have held about ourselves and the world around us, Reiki is simple and using it is not complicated.

Any time and for every situation, Reiki is there for you. The wisdom of your bodymind will use Reiki to get to the root of the imbalance and help you to heal on all levels. If you are feeling tired or have pain, take time to draw in Reiki energy.

If you are among a group of people and feel you are absorbing their emotions and energy, focus on drawing in Reiki energy until your body is full and beaming it. When you are feeling off-center, draw in Reiki energy and allow it to ground you to the earth.

Perform Reiki every day on yourself to recharge your energy. Like a vehicle, our bodies need to be maintained and not ignored until problems, anxiety or illnesses arise. Every time you use Reiki on yourself, you are releasing beliefs, energy and memories that are dulling your natural, perfect state of being. With those releases, your frequency will be raised to where it is meant to be. This can help you to see your true purpose as well as the connections and miracle that is your life.

As mentioned, performing Reiki first thing in the morning can set your frequency for the day ahead. It is thought that our subconscious is especially receptive just as we wake up. Performing a self-treatment and bringing to mind how you want to feel and how you want your day to proceed can be extremely powerful. Also, a self-treatment before you go to sleep can help you to relax and unwind, as well as helping you process the day's events, emotions and energy leading to a restful night of sleep.

Benefits of Daily Self-Treatments

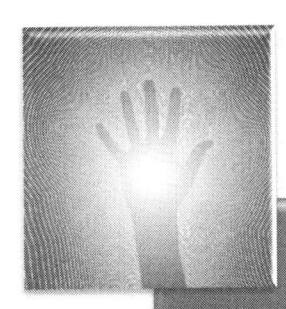

What Reiki Can Do For You

- Reiki will help you to relax
- Reiki helps to bring clarity
- Reiki energizes you
- Reiki calms you
- Reiki helps you to solve problems
- Reiki relieves pain
- Reiki accelerates natural healing
- Reiki helps prevents the progress of disease
- Reiki detoxifies the body
- Reiki dissolves energy blockages
- Reiki releases emotional baggage
- Reiki increases the vibrational frequency of the body
- Reiki helps change negative conditioning & behaviour

How to Perform Self-Treatments

When starting out you may worry if you are "doing it right". There is no single physical correct way to perform Reiki. In the beginning, you will likely begin with a set routine but over time, with confidence you will use your intuition and move your hands accordingly. Although we do not focus on the symptoms, if you are experiencing symptoms in a specific area, you can place your hands directly over that area at the start of the session, and continue with the remaining hand positions.

Some students ask, if Reiki goes where needed, why are there hand positions at all? If a practitioner is choosing to limit their hand positions, there may be some resistance on a conscious level which could impact the flow of energy. This is not always the case the but what is important is that the practitioner is open to performing all hand positions as needed. I have found that clients do like the physical sensations they experience and having all of the hand positions makes them feel as though all parts of the body were addressed so they are also in place to ease the recipient's mind even though energetically the body is diverting the energy as it needs to.

Even once you are experienced, check in once in a while to ensure your self-treatments are addressing all areas and aspects of the body. Sometimes we may subconsciously avoid an area of our body without realizing it so you may find it helpful to perform a complete self-treatment with additional hand positions as needed every so often.

In the beginning, you will find it helpful to use the positions listed below. When you have mastered those hand positions you can then allow your intuition to guide your self-treatments. You may wish to play music during your self-treatments. Try to perform your self-treatments in a place where you will not be disturbed and feel comfortable. Generally, try to spend a minimum of three to five minutes in each position. You can spend more time in areas as needed.

You will always hear, a little Reiki is better than none at all so if your time is limited, do what you can. It is better to spend a shorter amount of time in each position rather than removing a specific position just to ensure your intent to address the entire bodymind is clear.

At the start of each self-treatment, set the intention that you are ready to heal and balance on all levels. When performing self-treatments, you can focus on your breath and with every inhale draw in Reiki energy. With every exhale, release any energy that is not serving you. In the gaps between your breaths, be present and observe the energy.

When you have finished your self-treatment drink a large glass of water. Working with energy can demand a bit more water. Close your eyes, focus on your breath and set the intention that the session is completed and give thanks. You may feel light headed, and if you need to rest, or sit down for a short time, allow yourself to do so. It is common to fall asleep during a self-treatment. If you do so, at your next self-treatment resume in the position you remember completing last and complete the self-treatment.

If you feel a specific area of your body needs more attention, even after you have completed a full self-treatment, listen to your bodymind and perform additional Reiki in that area.

Self-Treatment Hand Positions

There is not an exact number of hand positions for Reiki self-treatments. The following hand positions are a starting point. Trust Reiki and your intuition.

After completing the positions, you may find that completing your treatment by placing your hands on each chakra starting at your root chakra and ending with your crown chakra beneficial.

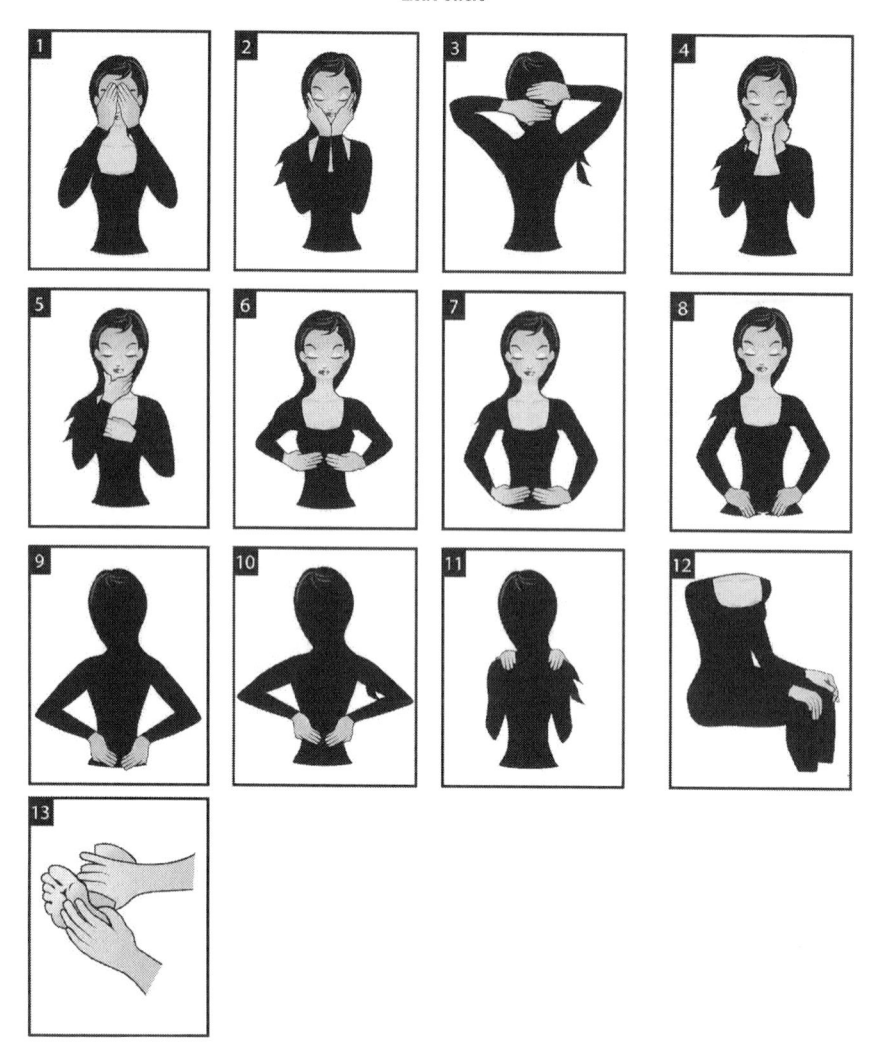

Performing Reiki on Yourself Consistently

You may find that as time goes by, your commitment to performing Reiki on yourself will wane. This is common and unfortunate. In order to heal the world, you must begin with yourself. Remember (this will be repeated again and again) that Reiki is not only a tool for balancing but also for increasing awareness. Healing and growth can occur spontaneously but more often they require dedicated focus and consistency in order to shift. In our society we gravitate towards immediate gratification, hoping for a quick fix or a magic red pill to change our reality. Reiki can be that solution but it will take time and require maintenance.

Just as you practice self-care such as bathing and flossing for your physical body, you must incorporate Reiki into your daily routine to cleanse and balance your energetic body.

The normal excuses such as a lack of time or energy is a reflection of beliefs around self-worth and the benefits of Reiki. Your health, vitality and consciousness are worth more than anything else. We are on this earth to experience everything life has to offer, positive and negative. Reiki helps us to use every situation as an opportunity to become better people and to raise our consciousness. Reiki can only serve us if we use it.

As with everything in life, the amount and type of energy you put into something is in direct proportion to what you will receive in return. By dedicating time for yourself and your well-being every day, miracles will occur. This time needs to be seen as a reward and a worthy pursuit.

Performing Reiki with Others

Where You Perform Reiki

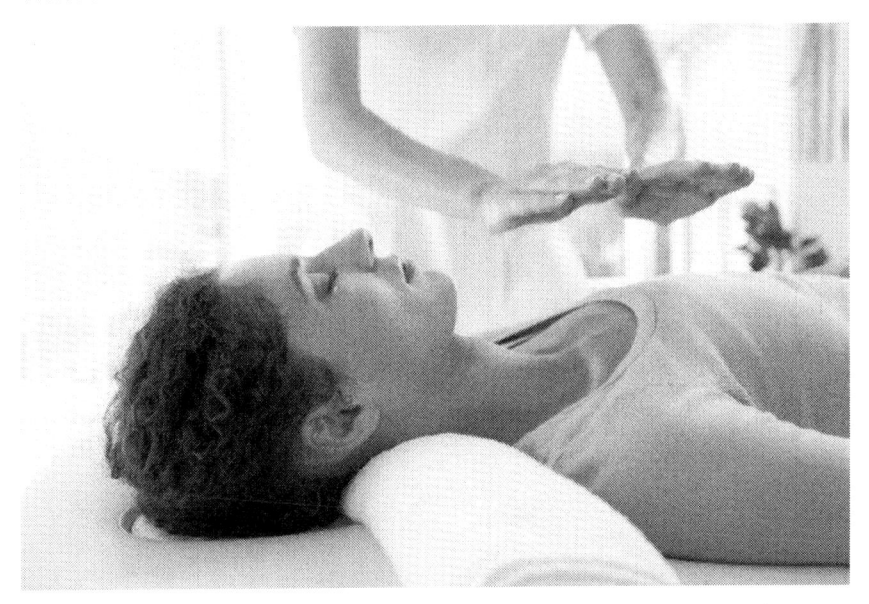

Although you can perform Reiki anywhere, ideally you choose a location that is relaxing and conducive to healing. Many practitioners perform Reiki in their home and have a room dedicated to their Reiki sessions. If this is not an option for you, you may want to consider joining a local centre such as a chiropractor's office or health focused store where you can rent a therapy room at a reasonable rate. Some offices will take a percentage of your session fees. This is beneficial when starting out but can add up once you have a full client list.

You will decorate your Reiki room in a way that feels right for you. Generally, the room should feel relaxing and clean, and be a safe space for you and your clients. Try to ensure your sessions will not be interrupted by distractions if you are working from home, such as the telephone or doorbell.

It is ideal to use a massage table when performing sessions. Using a couch or chair can be uncomfortable for you as the practitioner which may take your focus away from the sessions. It is common practice to use two pillows, one for the client's head and other for under their knees. Make sure the temperature of your Reiki room is comfortable. Some people may get cold during the session so having a blanket at their feet that they can pull up is handy.

Try not to have clutter in the room as that can store energy which can impact the tone of the session. Some practitioners like to have silence during a session while others prefer to have soft music playing in the background. Music can help you as the practitioner to relax and allow you to focus on the session. Try to avoid music that is popular and the client will recognize as they could have associations with the music that may not be conducive to the session.

There is music available that has been created specifically for bodywork and Reiki sessions. The tracks usually play for 45-60 minutes and include a bell or chime added at regular intervals to let you know when to move your hands.

Some practitioners choose to burning essential oils. Please be aware that some people are sensitive to certain smells and it may distract them from the session and even lead to a negative experience. Always ask your client before you begin using the scents.

Crying before, during and after a Reiki session can occur as your client releases blocked emotional issues and energy, so you will want to have a box of tissues close during the client intake and session. If at any point you start to feel the emotions your client is experiencing, take a deep breath, center yourself and focus on the Reiki energy. The flow of Reiki is one way only through you, drawn in by the recipient.

Preparing for a Session

Reiki is not limited by time or space and can travel through all materials such as stone and metal. However, our jewellery connects with the energy of the person wearing it and can store that energy. This energy can serve as blocks to healing. It is advisable to remove all jewellery such as rings, watches, earrings, chains and necklaces from yourself and ask your client to remove any jewellery as well.

Practitioners who work with precious stones and crystals for healing purposes, understand that these materials can become saturated with negative energy. That is why they cleanse them frequently.

If as a practitioner you find yourself resistant to removing any form of jewellery, try cleansing it frequently and see if that resistance releases. In many cases the resistance to remove jewellery is due to beliefs that are connected to the jewellery.

This connection can be made in many ways. A significant event may have occurred and somehow the beliefs and energy connected with that event are also stored in the jewellery. The jewellery may have been gifted or passed down from someone else with a specific energetic signature. Body piercings for the sake of convenience do not need to be removed but it is interesting to note that the act of body piercing can be comparable to a form of self-acupuncture and with balancing through Reiki, the individual may no longer feel called to keep in the piercings.

The energy flows within and along the outside of our body. To ensure that the energy flows without restriction, the client should have on loose clothing and their shoes off. Tightly fitted items can serve to block the flow of energy along significant energy pathways. Reiki is always performed with clothes on.

As the practitioner you will also want to make sure that your clothes are comfortable so you can focus on the session rather than physical sensations such as discomfort.

Alcohol reduces energy and lowers your frequency. Do not consume alcohol or any recreational mind-altering substances for twenty-four hours before a session. Medications prescribed by your doctor are acceptable.

Ensure you are clean and free of smells including perfume/cologne. You may wish to rinse your mouth or use breath mints before a session. Remember that you will be in close contact with your client for approximately an hour so you want that hour to be focused on the Reiki and not on you.

Always wash your hands before each Reiki session. This is for hygienic reasons but can also serve a purpose in grounding you and releasing excess energy in preparation for your session.

Setting your Intention

Remember that as a Reiki practitioner **you are not the one doing the healing**. The recipient of the Reiki energy is drawing it in and is healing themselves. **You are the conduit that enables them to draw the Reiki energy to the places in their body that are ready to be balanced**. Setting this intention will serve as a reminder that you are a witness and not actively doing anything. As a practitioner, you are at your strongest when you are being, not doing.

Although setting an intention is not essential to performing a powerful Reiki session, it is an effective way to disengage from your ego and expectations around the outcome and become present.

You may wish to also energetically ask for permission to perform a Reiki session on the recipient so that they may heal and balance on all levels. You do not have to say your intention out loud, you can just pause for a moment before you begin your session and set your intention.

An example of the intention you can set could resemble the following:

I am open to receiving Reiki energy and allowing (recipient's name) to draw in the Reiki energy that is needed so that they may balance on all levels for their highest good and the highest good of all concerned. May we all be empowered by love and light.

This can be done while standing at the head of your client or beside them. You will take a few deep breaths and set your intention before you begin.

Working with the Aura

You may find it helpful to do a general clearing of your client's aura; the energy surrounding their body, before beginning your Reiki session. You would very slowly and smoothly run your hands above the recipient's body (six inches or higher) along the aura from the head down to their feet in a sweeping motion. This can be completed a few times to remove any external energy that is being stored and is ready to release. You can pay attention to the sensations in your hands as you do this and use your intuition to sense for areas that you may wish to focus on during your Reiki session.

Considerations When Working with Others

Before you begin a complete Reiki session on another person there are some important things you will want to consider.

Although there have been no medical studies to validate this, practitioners generally tend to avoid performing Reiki close to a pacemaker. A pacemaker is an electronic device that regulates the heart rate in an individual. These individuals are counselled to stay away from sources of energy such as microwaves and metal detectors in airports. It has been measure that the energy emitted from a practitioner's hands is greater than that of a non-practitioner so the notion to avoid performing Reiki on the heart center of an individual with a pacemaker is to ensure that the energy from the practitioner's hands does not interfere with the signals the pacemaker provides.

When working with individuals with pacemakers, you can complete a session without focusing on the heart center with the understanding that if the heart area is in need of balancing, the bodymind of the recipient will draw energy into that area. You can also perform distance sessions with these individuals.

When you are working with individuals who are on medications, you will want to let them know that it is important that they monitor their body and see their doctor if they notice shifts in their physical state. The doctor can then re-evaluate and adjust medications as necessary. This is especially important with regard to individuals who are taking insulin for diabetes (type I and II). The body can balance blood sugar levels rapidly and if the person is not frequently checking their levels, they may administer an overdose of insulin. Any worries can be avoided as long as the recipient is aware that they need to be diligent and pay attention to their blood sugar levels and condition to ensure that they are giving themselves the correct dose of medication.

It is recommended that you have your client complete a form that outlines all of their physical and emotional conditions. This will help you monitor the client's progress.

You will want to provide new clients with a brief introduction to Reiki and explain exactly what a Reiki session looks like. You can also explain the types of sensations they may experience. Remember to let your clients know that any one of these reactions are normal and that their body decides what is being balanced and when. Remind them that their body is in control. Some clients may experience any of the following:

Reactions that may occur

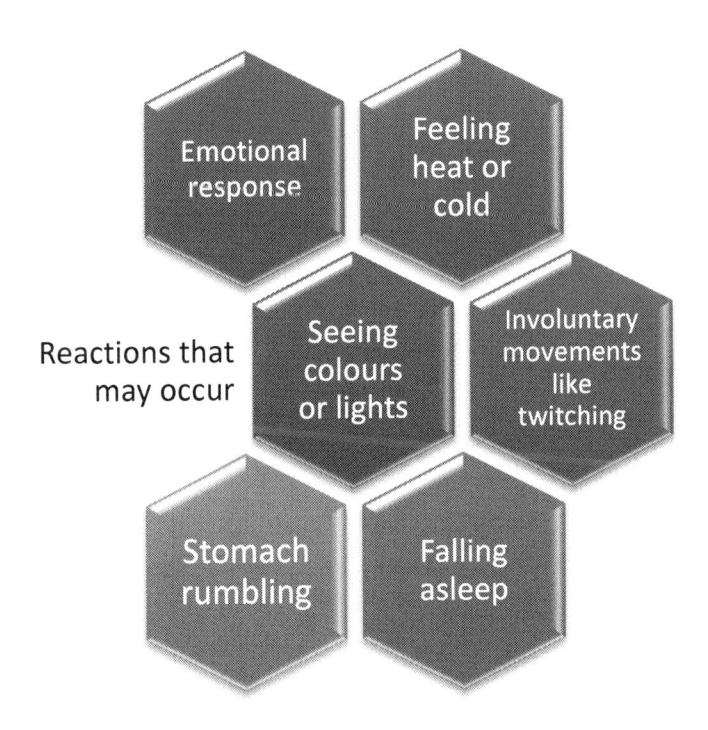

- Emotional response
- Feeling heat or cold
- Seeing colours or lights
- Involuntary movements like twitching
- Stomach rumbling
- Falling asleep

If the client does not experience anything eventful during the session, you can explain that because the body decides what to balance and when, and that shifts can occur solely on an energetic level at first but over time can have physical results as well. This is where having a detailed client intake will be helpful. When things improve, we tend to forget about them. Going through the intake at the start of each session will show you and your client how things are shifting.

When you first begin working with others, you can get caught up in whether you are performing sessions correctly and if your sessions are "working". Again it is important to remember that the client is drawing in Reiki energy through you. The recipient is doing the work to balance themselves and you are the conduit and observer.

Remember that the bodymind will draw Reiki energy to what is ready to be balanced and in the correct order that will best benefit the client. No knowledge of the human anatomy or physiology is required to work with Reiki. Your only job is to BE, not DO.

Although it is helpful to have an understanding of what imbalances the client is aware of at the start of the session, once you begin release the labels and judgements and just observe the energy. In many cases, imbalances with symptoms in one area of the body have additional and connected imbalances in other areas. Sense the different types of energy as you go through each position. You will find you develop your own way of deciphering whether to stay in a position longer than others. Some practitioners find they feel the energy is weaker, while others find the energy is stronger. You will create your own way of navigating through a session.

Prescribing and Diagnosing

A diagnosis is a label to describe a symptom or collection of symptoms. This helps our linear minds process information for classification purposes. Then based on this diagnosis, a prescription of things that may have worked to some degree for others with similar symptoms is given. Here is where things can fall out of order.

Let's say for example that you have back pain. And let's also say that your friend has back pain. It is reasonable to assume that the cause of your back pain is likely different than what is causing your friend's back pain. Yet in many modalities what are addressed are the symptoms (back pain) rather than what is causing the back pain.

So if the cause of similar symptoms is completely different, then treating according to the symptoms will not yield the same results as treating the source of the condition. Makes sense?

In a Reiki session, we always want to allow the body to work with the root cause of the imbalance rather than the symptoms. One of the many things that make Reiki so powerful is that the practitioner does not diagnose or prescribe.

Our perception is completely unique and is a reflection of our own personal beliefs, memories and genetic make-up. These things filter our experience and are the glasses that we see our world through.

As a Reiki practitioner, we understand our perception is biased and work with releasing the filters that limit our experience, but we also ensure that we do not limit the experience of our sessions with those filters by clearing our mind and keeping our ego out of it.

The underlying assumption with Reiki is that the body knows how to heal itself. Just as you generate new lungs every 6 weeks and a new liver every 5 months, your body is capable of creating a new healthy you. Reiki energy helps the body to release the energy that is preventing it from doing its job of maintaining balance.

In a Reiki session although there are hand positions, these are fluid and the practitioner knows that the body of the recipient is drawing in the energy to the specific areas within that require it. I am often asked by new students – "what are the hand positions for diabetes?" or "how do I perform a Reiki session on someone with cancer?" Over time, they learn that the answer is – you always provide a complete Reiki session.

Practitioners of other modalities may argue that the physical symptoms are usually traced back to an energetic imbalance which can be addressed by focusing on specific chakras or meridians and provide specific hand positions and treatments for such. In some cases, the session may be somewhat effective but if they truly worked for most people, these prescriptive treatments would be the standard of care across all modalities. We know this is not the case and in many instances is one way a modality or even practitioner has tried to ineffectively be distinguished from the rest. Reiki practitioners see the best results from their sessions because they do not limit their work based on a one size fits all approach.

As our understanding of our bodies deepen, including how our memories are stored and the genetic memory we carry with us from birth, we know that a single belief can wreak havoc on the physical body. That energy which can be stored in a single cell, can impact all aspects of physiology and anatomy of its hosting body.

By keeping our ego's desire to figure out what is imbalanced, and trusting that the recipient's body knows what it is doing, healing will occur. By allowing the recipient to subconsciously choose what is addressed and when, the power to control and heal lies exactly where it should be – in the recipient. Every day I am so grateful to be able to perform Reiki and teach to others the understanding that the power to heal ourselves and our lives truly lies within each of us.

Beginning The Reiki Session

You will begin the session with your client lying down comfortably on the table face up, fully clothed with their arms at their sides. Their legs should be relaxed and flat against the table and not be crossed as this can interrupt the flow of energy like crossing two electrical wires.

As a practitioner you may either perform the session with your hands directly on the body of the recipient or slightly above their body. Both ways are effective so this may be determined by the regulations in your area, your preferences and the preferences of your client. You will gently and slowly place your hands on or above the body and ensure the shift from position to position is slow and smooth.

For injured or sensitive areas such as the face, throat, chest and genitals, you will NOT want to place your hands directly on the client. In those areas, hold your hands approximately 4-5 inches above the body. For clients with touch issues you can perform the entire session with your hands above the client's body rather than in contact with it. You can confirm your client's preferences during the intake. Keep your hands in each position for between three to five minutes. As you become more experienced you will use your intuition to guide you regarding the length of time you spend in each position.

Your fingers should be held together when your hands are in position. This keeps the channel strong between your client and the universal life force.

Pay attention to non-verbal communication from your client's body. Deep sighs or hand and leg movements are good indicators that something positive is taking place. Generally, a full session is between forty-five to sixty minutes.

One question often asked is: if Reiki has infinite wisdom and will be drawn where it is needed, why do we have to use hand positions. Can we for example just place our hands on the head for the entire session?

The answer to this question has a slight variation when we consider working with others.

Intention is key as the practitioner and sometimes inadvertently we may avoid certain locations with the client as a result of our own imbalances. The hand positions ensure that our intention is to allow Reiki to flow through the entire bodymind of the recipient.

Also, from a client's perspective, typically they like to feel that their entire bodymind is being addressed and the physical sensation that they receive from the hand positions gives their conscious mind that understanding.

Although some practitioners like to have their clients roll over mid session, I prefer to keep my clients on their backs. In many cases a client is so relaxed and even sleeping during the session so to have them roll over can disrupt the energy flow. Because Reiki flows through the body, you can place your hands above the front of it while setting the intention that the position is intended for the back of the client.

At the end of a session always offer your client a glass of cold water to aid in grounding. You will also want to wash your hands in cold water after each session. This will help your bodymind feel that the session has ended.

Full Body Hand Positions

Remember that the following hand positions are only a guide. Use your intuition

Closing the Session

When you have completed all hand positions, there are a couple of ways you can finish your session. Some practitioners place one hand on their client's crown chakra and the other hand above the client's root chakra. Another option which I like is to place one hand on the crown chakra and the other on the heart chakra. This final position can help to balance the energy and close the session.

Just as you began the session, you may also want to complete your session by sweeping your client's aura. This is done by moving your hands slowly in a sweeping motion above the recipient's body from their head to feet and can be repeated a few times or as necessary.

Once the session is finished, you can gently let the recipient know the session is complete and give them a few minutes to get up. During that time, you can get them a glass of cold water as well as wash your hands and drink some water.

When we are running energy through our bodies, our awareness can shift to the higher energetic frequencies which can make us less present in our physical reality. Running your hands under the water and drinking cold water can help us to resume our focus to the here and now which is helpful when we resume our daily activities.

Time Constraints

If time does not permit you to perform a complete Reiki session, you can use the time you have to perform an abbreviated version. Completing the hand positions for each chakra as well as the elbows, hands, knees and feet can be effective. The recipient can be seated in a chair if a treatment table is not available. This session can take as little as fifteen minutes and although it is not as thorough as a complete session, it is much better than no session at all. You can then close this quick session by sweeping the recipient's aura. You will still want to offer the recipient water as well as washing your hands in cold water once the session has ended.

Group Reiki Sessions

Group sessions are thought to be first used by Dr Hayashi in his clinic in Tokyo. These would be conducted by performing sessions with clients with the help of several other Reiki practitioners. Some people find it enjoyable to work with others and there are some advantages to working in a group.

Group sessions are faster than a traditional session, taking around ten minutes to complete. Group sessions can also be very powerful with the client receiving energy from multiple channels. Group sessions can also help practitioners to form a bond with one another as they work together.

You will prepare for a group session as you would a traditional session. Before you begin, as a group you will decide who will work on each position as well as who will end the session by sweeping the recipient's aura. If you do not have enough practitioners for each hand position, you will spend 3-5 minutes at each position and then rotate in a clockwise or counter-clockwise direction (depending on what the group decides). Generally, the individual who begins the group session working on the recipient's head will dictate when the hand placement is changed. Remember to wash your hands before and after each session under cold running water to assist grounding for each member of the team.

This is a great way to perform Reiki on many people in a short amount of time. In many cities, there are what is called "Reiki Shares" where practitioners meet regularly to give and receive Reiki. In many cases, Reiki Shares include group sessions where practitioners work with each other.

Reiki and Pregnancy, Babies & Children

Reiki is safe and can be very beneficial for a pregnant woman and her child. Reiki can be used to help:

Using Reiki during and after Pregnancy
- Reduce fatigue
- Stimulate healthy development
- Address pain
- Facilitate a connection between mother and child
- Reduce post-partum depression
- Accelerate healing after delivery
- Milk production or formula absorbtion
- Balance colic

Reiki can also help prepare for conception by reducing stress and stimulating the reproductive cycles of the couple. Important Note: Always consult your doctor no matter what if you are concerned about you or your baby.

Instinctively we kiss or touch our children when they hurt themselves. Reiki is an extension of that action. You can perform

Reiki on your children from the time they are born. Most children are very sensitive to energy and love the sensation. Meditating on the 5 principles with your children can also be very beneficial.

With each session, children become more familiar with the energy and may even be able to tell you when they feel things shifting. Reiki is also a wonderful way to connect with children who are non-verbal.

Reiki and Palliative Care

Depending on what culture you were raised in will determine how you view death. Some cultures see death as the end where other cultures view it as a new beginning. Regardless, death is something we all must face. Reiki can help assist those who are dying and preparing to leave this physical plane. Reiki can also be used to help those grieving the loss of loved ones. Reiki can help ensure that the grieving process is flowing and that emotions are being processed and released rather than resisted and stored.

Thanatology (the study of death and the dying) strives to provide insight into what happens after death. There are many reports that point to the notion that there is life after death.

If you plan to work with individuals who are dying or grieving loss, you will want to examine your beliefs and conduct the research you need to provide evidence for yourself either way. Resolving any conflict, you have around the concept of death will ensure you are a clear channel for Reiki energy during your sessions.

During a Reiki session both the practitioner and recipient have a strong connection with the universal life force. Many recipients find that sessions help them have the strength to resolve unfinished business they have and find resolution with regard to previous conflicts. I have also found that Reiki sessions can help the recipient have a peaceful transition.

Conclusion

You have now completed Level I and hopefully this course has opened a new world for you. You now have the skills to perform Reiki effectively on yourself and others. Many individuals find that this course material is all they need to create and maintain balance and harmony in their lives. Remember that Reiki is not only meant to heal but to increase awareness as well.

It is my hope that you use Reiki in your life each day to make it the best life possible.

Love and light,

Lisa

Reiki Level II

招福の秘法
萬病の霊薬
今日丈けは　怒るな
心配すな　感謝して
業をはけめ　人に親切に
朝夕合掌して心に念じ
口に唱へよ
心身改善臼井霊氣療法
　　　肇祖
　　　　臼井甕男

Level I Review

You will remember from Reiki Level I that Reiki is different from other healing modalities because practitioners are initiated through an attunement. The Reiki Master uses the power of the Reiki symbols to attune the practitioner to Reiki energy. This has been done since the founder, Mikao Usui attuned his first student. Although we are all natural healers, Reiki helps us to fine tune these abilities. Another factor that distinguishes Reiki from other healing arts is that although the Reiki energy transmits through the practitioner into the receiver, it does not originate from the practitioner. A Reiki attunement lasts for life.

The secret method of inviting blessings

The spiritual medicine of many illnesses

For today only do not anger, do not worry

Be grateful and

Do your work with appreciation

Be kind to all living things

In the morning and at night

with hands held in prayer

Think this in your mind

chant this with your mouth
The Usui Reiki Method to change your mind and body for the better

We will review the Reiki principles, the spiritual basis of the Usui Reiki System. In level I you were taught the 5 Principles of the Meiji Emperor that Usui adopted into the Reiki system. These principles were to be said morning and night to help you focus on the universal source of light, love and harmony that is Reiki.

If you have been working with the principles each morning and evening, you may have noticed that they have had a positive effect on you. When said often, they help the mind to focus on your life purpose, awakening, gratitude, and compassion for all.

Many people begin to see a pattern emerging in their actions. At first you may react as you always have based on the ego and its conditioning. Yet as you practice the principles, they slowly become a part of your conscious mind. Then when something negative happens you may still react, but afterwards remember the principles and establish control. As time passes you will find that as you are reacting you remember the principles and begin to react less. Over time you become aware of the pattern and its purpose and stop the reaction earlier and earlier in the cycle. Finally, you are free of that conditioning and prefer to respond to the situation in a calm and peaceful manner.

Reiki Level II

Reiki Level II will help you to deepen your understanding of this amazing modality. It is likely that by the time you are studying at this level, your doubt and scepticism regarding the effectiveness of Reiki has fallen away and you have a deep respect for the results that Reiki can provide on physical, mental, emotional and energetic levels. If you are feeling called to complete this level, you are ready.

Like most things involving energy, learning is experiential. You can effort to try to understand how Reiki energy works and science is providing much more information to help us intellectually navigate through it but the best way to understand Reiki energy is by feeling it.

Reiki energy is everywhere and in all things. It connects everything and has a consciousness that allows everything to be in a constant state of communication.

Morphic resonance is a concept you may find interesting to investigate and involves the notion that inherited memory can be transmitted in ways other than genetics. Rupert Sheldrake has spent considerable time researching this phenomenon.

If you are interested in exploring the science behind Reiki, you can explore quantum physics. In his work, Deepak Chopra has also taken more complex scientific discoveries and translated them into easy to understand packets of information.

Reiki Level II will continue to explore the amazing power of Reiki.

Applications for Reiki Level II

The second degree explores the Reiki symbols and teaches you how to use them. These symbols will help you to magnify and focus the Reiki energy.

The use of these symbols can help to accelerate a session, perform a session from a distance or on imbalances from the past or future as well as focus on mental and emotional clearing. As you use the symbols you will find more applications for them in your sessions and life. With the Level II attunement, your body's frequency and psychic perception will be heightened.

Reiki Symbols

Symbols have been used for centuries to convey messages and when used by large groups can hold a specific vibration. Sacred geometry is one example of such symbols.

The symbols are another aspect of Reiki that sets it apart from other healing modalities. Although practitioners can effectively utilize

Reiki energy without the use of the symbols, the symbols help to amplify and refine the energy during a session.

There are four sacred symbols Dr. Mikao Usui taught his students and attuned them to. Three symbols are taught in Level II with the fourth symbol being taught to students in the Master Level.

Like being attuned to Reiki, once a student has been attuned to the Reiki symbols; they will be connected to those symbols for life. As your understanding of the Reiki symbols deepen through use, you will be able to determine for yourself how you will use the symbols in your practice and life.

The Reiki symbols can only be used for a positive outcome. During the attunement ceremony, the Reiki Master connects the Reiki student, Reiki energy and the symbols. From that point on, the student will draw on the intentions of the symbols to channel Reiki energy at an amplified rate. The student needs to be attuned to the symbols in order to connect with their power. Being attuned to the symbols means that once the student begins using the symbols, they will have that connection in place.

Usui found the four symbols in Sanskrit sutras he was studying and although he did not initially use them in his sessions, Usui realized that the symbols would help align students to Reiki energy in a more specific way. The symbols can be used when working with others or self.

The intention that is held when using the symbols is very important. You may find it helpful to visualize the symbols as live energy. You may see colors when using the symbols such as white. You can draw the symbols in your mind and see them placed above various parts of the body of the recipient.

Cho Ku Rei - The Power Symbol

CHO KU REI

The first symbol is the Cho Ku Rei pronounced cho-koo-ray and means "Placing the power of the universe here". It is the power symbol and considered an amplifier. This symbol is sometimes referred to as the "light switch" because it powers on and activates the other symbols. The counter-clockwise spiral in this symbol is thought to dis-create imbalance by helping to release dissonant energy so the true resonance of the recipient can shine through. The intention of this symbol is immediately cutting through the illusion of imbalance and releasing it using the power of the universe.

The Cho Ku Rei symbol can be used alone or as an activator for some of the other symbols. Reiki's infinite wisdom will bring about whatever is needed.

Cho Ku Rei is either written as 勅令 (imperial edict) or 直靈 (direct spirit) in Chinese.

How to draw the Cho-Ku-Rei

1. Draw a horizontal line from left to right.
2. Beginning at the right side of Line 1, draw a vertical line from top to bottom.
3. Draw a counter-clockwise spiral with 3.5 turns.

How to Use the Symbols

The Reiki power symbol can be used to connect with Reiki energy at the beginning of a session, to activate the other symbols and also to help boost the power of the energy when required during a session.

> ### Ways to Use the Symbols
> - Mentally beam a white (CKR, SHK, HSZSN) through your hands as you work with a client
> - Visualize white symbol (CKR, SHK, HSZSN) on the palms of your hands before your session
> - Draw the symbol (CKR, SHK, HSZSN) with your tongue on the roof of your mouth and project it on the back of your hands as you perform your session
> - Draw the symbol (CKR, SHK, HSZSN) on your hands with your index finger before you begin your session
> - Draw the symbol (CKR, SHK, HSZSN) in the air and beam it in the direction of your hands
>
> CHO KU REI

Important Note – Although it is traditional practice to not allow anyone to observe you drawing the symbols unless they are a second degree practitioner or a Reiki master if you feel called to display the symbols you can do so. In the past the symbols were kept hidden but they are now available to everyone who performs an internet search Unless they are attuned, the power of the symbols is not available to them so there is no need to worry.

When using the symbol, you will want to silently say the words Cho Ku Rei three times as you draw it. The silent intonation helps to strengthen the intention. If you have a difficult situation, you may find it helpful to write the problem down on a piece of paper and draw the Cho Ku Rei symbol over the top of the writing. You can then hold the paper and allow the situation to draw Reiki energy in.

Ways you can use the Cho Ku Rei (CKR) symbol

- Activates the other symbols.
- For protection
- Bring resolution
- Cleanse
- Bring balance
- Drawn under a stamp on a letter.
- Placed under a sticker on a gift.
- Used on your food, drink, plants, animals etc.
- For your career, draw it on your desk, under the cash register, on documents, letters, the telephone, your diary, computer etc.
- Can be beamed on airlines, trains, pilots, drivers etc.
- In your home, can be drawn invisibly under your doormat, under wallpaper, in cupboards, behind pictures etc.
- Anything else you can imagine

Sei He Ki - The Emotional Healing Symbol

SEI HE KI

The second symbol is the Sei He Ki pronounced say-hay-key. Sei He Ki is thought to work on an emotional level and balance the two hemispheres of the brain. One translation of this means: The earth and sky meet *or* God and Man become one. In essence the Sei He Ki holds the resonance of creating through balance.

How to draw the Sei-He Ki

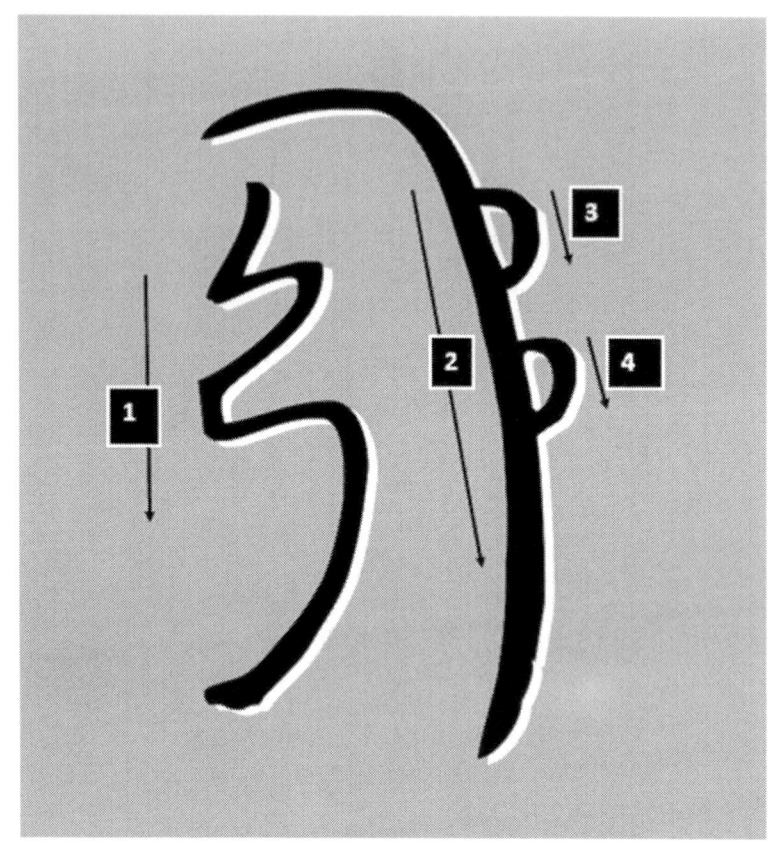

1. Draw a three part curved line.

2. Draw a single curved line from top to bottom.

3 & 4. Draw two half-circles.

Ways you can use the Sei He Ki (SHK) symbol

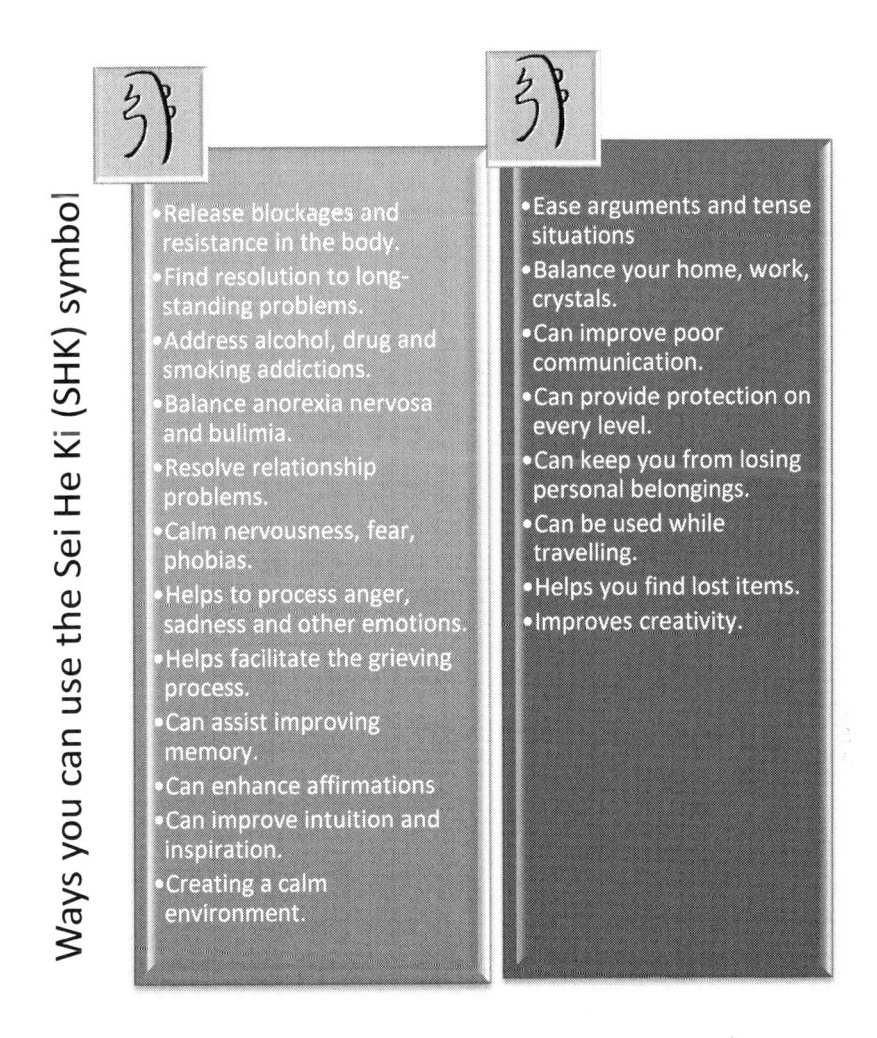

- Release blockages and resistance in the body.
- Find resolution to long-standing problems.
- Address alcohol, drug and smoking addictions.
- Balance anorexia nervosa and bulimia.
- Resolve relationship problems.
- Calm nervousness, fear, phobias.
- Helps to process anger, sadness and other emotions.
- Helps facilitate the grieving process.
- Can assist improving memory.
- Can enhance affirmations
- Can improve intuition and inspiration.
- Creating a calm environment.

- Ease arguments and tense situations
- Balance your home, work, crystals.
- Can improve poor communication.
- Can provide protection on every level.
- Can keep you from losing personal belongings.
- Can be used while travelling.
- Helps you find lost items.
- Improves creativity.

To activate the Sei He Ki symbol you will draw the Cho Ku Rei symbol while intoning the words Cho Ku Rei three times to activate the SHK. Then draw the Sei He Ki on top of (or beside) the Cho Ku Rei and intone the words Sei He Ki three times. For additional energy you can also then draw the Cho Ku Rei on top of (or beside) the Sei He Ki while intoning the words Cho Ku Rei three times.

The Sei He Ki can be used to release beliefs that are preventing the person from balancing and healing.

You can visualise any of the symbols beaming out of your third eye chakra and entering the third eye chakra of the recipient. You can also draw the symbols on your hands and then place them over the clients' third eye chakra. The third eye chakra is used in this instance because the goal is to align the recipient with their insight and intuition so they can release what is not true and embrace the reality of their perfection. Using the Sei He Ki is often helpful when you are working with a person with addictions, those wanting weight loss or to release unwanted habits. You will want to be sure to keep a box of tissues nearby as this can often cause the client to become weepy and emotional.

You may find you feel called to use the Sei He Ki symbol at any time during your session.

If you are working with a person who is suffering from an imbalance such as cancer, or other immune system disorders, you can visualize Sei He Ki symbols penetrating every cell in the body of the recipient. When you have an issue you need more clarity on or you are seeking a solution, write it down on a piece of paper and draw the Reiki symbols shown below either on top of the problem or beside it. Be open to receiving a solution.

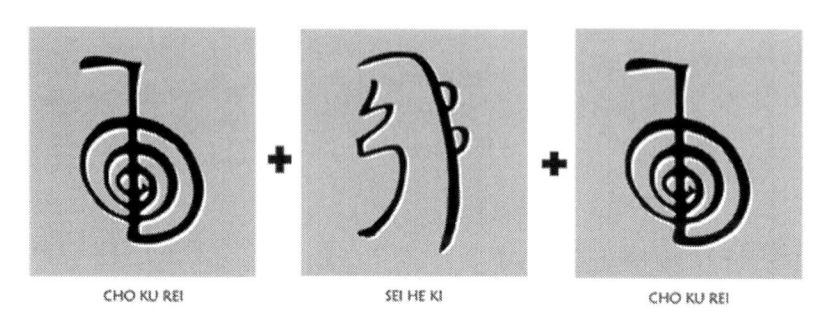

CHO KU REI + SEI HE KI + CHO KU REI

Hon Sha Ze Sho Nen - The Distance Symbol

The Hon Sha Ze Sho Nen (HSZSN) symbol is known as the distance healing symbol, and is used to transcend time and space with one translation being 'having no past, present or future'. The Cho Ku Rei symbol is used first to activate the Hon Sha Ze Sho Nen. **(Note: although it is spoken Hon Sha Ze Sho Nen, the kanji Sho is written before Ze).**

The HSZSN gives the Reiki practitioner the ability to channel Reiki across short or long distances

The HSZSN also allows the practitioner to travel time from the present to the past or future. Reiki can be used to balance issues from years past and even work with karmic or past life issues. Future situations such as medical interventions, interviews or important events can be balanced by performing Reiki before they occur. In some cases, an individual's body is not ready to balance in the present moment but may have a time in the future when it will feel safe to heal and when the balanced state will hold. For example, a woman in an abusive situation may not feel ready to heal until after she has been able to successfully release the relationship. The HSZSN symbol can be used to allow the body to draw in Reiki at that point in time with the outcome being that the woman will experience the effects of the balancing in the present.

TRANSCENDING TIME AND SPACE

HON

SHA

SHO

ZE

NEN

How to Draw the Hon-Sha-Ze-Sho-Nen Symbol

When the Hon-Sha-Ze-Sho-Nen symbol is drawn, all strokes are drawn from left to right and from top to bottom.

1. The first horizontal stroke means the number one, beginning, eternity beginning in this moment.
2. The second vertical stroke which crosses over the first, means the number ten, completion.

3/4. The third and fourth strokes are angled out and down and combined with strokes one and two symbolize a tree in Japanese. This can be translated into the tree of life, transformation, knowledge.

5. The fifth horizontal stroke means the root of the tree, cause, the origin.

   These strokes form the first kanji HON. (Kanji means Japanese writing using Chinese characters. Kan – Chinese, Ji – character).

6. The sixth horizontal stroke symbolizes earth.

7. Stroke seven is a downward curving line meaning to become.

8. Stroke eight is a vertical line drawn downwards from the curved line.

9. Stroke nine is a horizontal line drawn from left to right

10. Stroke ten is a horizontal line drawn from the end of stroke eight.

11. Stroke eleven is drawn from left to right underneath stroke 10.

    Strokes six through eleven form the Kanji SHA which means a person that creates. This symbol means what was hidden is brought into being. This relates to the miracle of Reiki. When you place your hands on someone, Reiki is revealing little by little what is already there.

12. Stroke number twelve is a horizontal line drawn from left to right. In some variations, this stroke is omitted.

13. Stroke number thirteen is a vertical line drawn from the center of stroke twelve.

14. Stroke number fourteen is a vertical line that is drawn to the left of stroke thirteen.

15. Stroke number fourteen is a small horizontal line that runs from the middle of line thirteen.

    Strokes numbered twelve to fifteen forms the kanji SHO meaning just and right.

16. Stroke number sixteen is a curved vertical line that angles down and outward to the left.

17. Stroke number seventeen is a curved vertical line that angles down and outward to the right.

   Strokes sixteen and seventeen combined form the kanji – ZE which means harmony and acting justly just as Reiki goes where it is needed.

   Note: Although the kanji ZE is drawn *after* the SHO, when speaking it out loud it is pronounced HON SHA ZE SHO NEN. Please see the diagram on the previous page to note the difference.

18. Stroke number eighteen is a short vertical line that angles to the right.
19. Stroke number nineteen is a longer horizontal line under lines sixteen and seventeen that curves under to the left.
20. Stroke twenty is a vertical curve similar to the letter c.
21/22. Strokes twenty-one and twenty-two are short vertical lines similar to eyes in a happy face. In some variations, these lines curve with 21 curving like a c and 22 curving in the opposite manner.

Strokes seventeen to twenty-two form the final kanji – NEN which translated can mean the heart, and in the now.

Please remember that the kanji are like forms of art. No two versions will be the same. Just as a calligrapher has a certain style and adds that to the lettering he/she does, the kanji are also very unique as each person draws them. Variations are acceptable. Try not to be consumed by the minute details and differences and instead focus on the resonance of the symbol.

How to Use the Hon-Sha-Ze-Sho-Nen Symbol

You will want to draw the Cho Ku Rei while intoning the words Cho Ku Rei three times to activate the Hon Sha Ze Sho Nen symbol. You then draw the Hon Sha Ze Sho Nen on top of the Cho Ku Rei (or beside it) and intone the words Hon Sha Ze Sho Nen three times. If you choose, you can then draw the Cho Ku Rei on top of the Hon

Sha Ze Sho Nen while intoning the words Cho Ku Rei three additional times.

> ### Examples of Uses for the HSZSN Symbol
> - Works with deep seated diseases and long term imbalances.
> - Transmits Reiki across distances near and far.
> - Works with groups, organizations, cities, countries etc.
> - Can help to prepare for events (interviews, tests, surgeries)
> - Can balance past life issues and memories.
> - Works with children while they rest.
> - Addresses imbalances from the past present and future.

You can also incorporate the HSZSN with the CKR and SHK (see illustration below). This complete formula would include the CKR, then SHK, CKR, then HSZSN, then CKR.

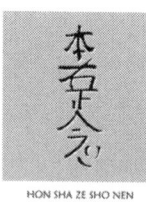

| CHO KU REI | SEI HE KI | CHO KU REI | HON SHA ZE SHO NEN | CHO KU REI |

How to Draw the Reiki Symbols

Cho Ku Rei – Power

Placing the power of the universe here

Sei He Ki – Emotional/Mental

Balance – the earth and sky meet

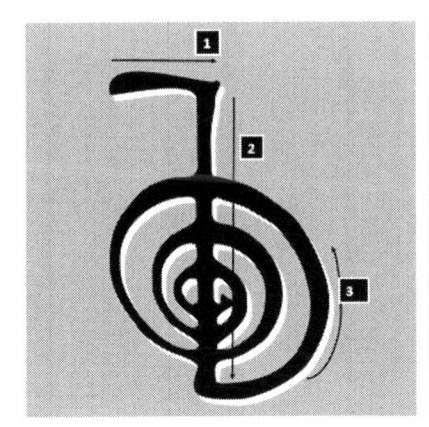

Hon Sha Ze Sho Nen – Distance

No past, present or future

TRANSCENDING TIME AND SPACE

HON

SHA

SHO

ZE

NEN

Gassho

You will use the three techniques to help deepen your work with the Reiki principles. These techniques are:

- Gassho: (Gash-Show)
- Reiji-Ho: (Ray-Gee-Hoe)
- Chiryo: (Chi-Rye-Oh)

Dr. Mikao Usui taught his students the Gassho meditation. The meaning of Gassho is "two hands coming together". Gassho helps one to hold the intention of gratitude and respect, focus, balance and connection to collective consciousness.

Students would place their hands in the Gassho position every morning and night. Gassho helps to focus and quiet the mind during meditation. This involves placing your hands in prayer position, closing your eyes, and bringing your awareness to the tip of your middle finger. If your mind wanders, gently press your middle fingers together and refocus.

There are two forms of the traditional Gassho, formal and informal.

Formal Gassho is used in rituals, religious services and formal gatherings to convey reverence. To perform Gassho you will bring your hands together with your palms facing each other and your fingers pointing to the sky. Your elbows will also be raised, with your forearms at a 30° angle to the floor. Your fingertips are at the height of your eyebrows, but your hands are about four inches away from the tip of your nose. Your eyes are focused on the tips of the middle fingers.

Mu-shin ('No-Mind') Gassho is a form of Gassho used mostly as a way of greeting others. The hands are held lightly together with the tips of the fingers and thumbs touching, and a little space between the palms of your hands. In this position, your forearms are at a 45° angle to the floor. You will hold your hands around four inches in front of your face (lower than the formal position), with your fingertips just below your nose. Again, the eyes are focused on the tips of your middle fingers. It is also common practice to perform mu-shin Gassho with hands positioned in front of the chest above the heart.

If you find this meditation beneficial, it is recommended that you perform it in the morning and evening for fifteen to thirty minutes ideally for one month. You may find it useful to make notes of your experiences as you meditate as well as how your life situation changes over time. You may find that you are more focused and grounded as each day passes.

Gassho Meditation

- In a seated position (on a chair or the floor), place your hands in mu-shin gassho position.
- Focus on where your two middle fingers meet.
- Let your thoughts fall away. As more thoughts arise, watch them go and keep your focus on your fingers.
- Recite the 5 Reiki principles or your version of them out loud or in your mind.
- If you find your arms getting uncomfortable you can slowly lower your hands to your lap.
- Watch the sensations you experience and allow those to fall away as well.
- When you are finished, send the intention of gratitude and end the session. You may find placing your palms on the ground an effective way to end the session and ground yourself.

Reiji-Ho

In English, Reiji means "indication of the Reiki energy." Ho means "technique." Reiji-Ho consists of three short rituals that can be performed before each Reiki session.

Step 1
- Hold your hands in front of your chest in the Gassho position with your eyes closed.
- Using the CKR and HSZN, ask that Reiki energy flow through you.
- Repeat this request three times.
- Invoke CKR and SHK to hold the intention.

Step 2
- Ask for the balancing of the client/recipient.
- Raise your hands to your third eye while keeping them in Gassho.
- Ask to have your hands guided to where Reiki energy is needed.

Step 3
- Allow this technique to guide your hands.
- Detach from any desires you have regarding the outcome of the session.
- Be open to receiving messages that will guide you.
- Your hands will rest when Reiji-Ho is complete. Perform Gassho one more time.
- Refrain from discussing specific areas or messages with your client.

Chiryo

In English, Chiryo means "treatment". Chiryo is performed by the practitioner holding their dominant hand above the client's crown chakra and waiting until there is a signal to move, which the hand then follows. The Reiki practitioner continues to use their intuition with regard to hand placement until they are called to end the session.

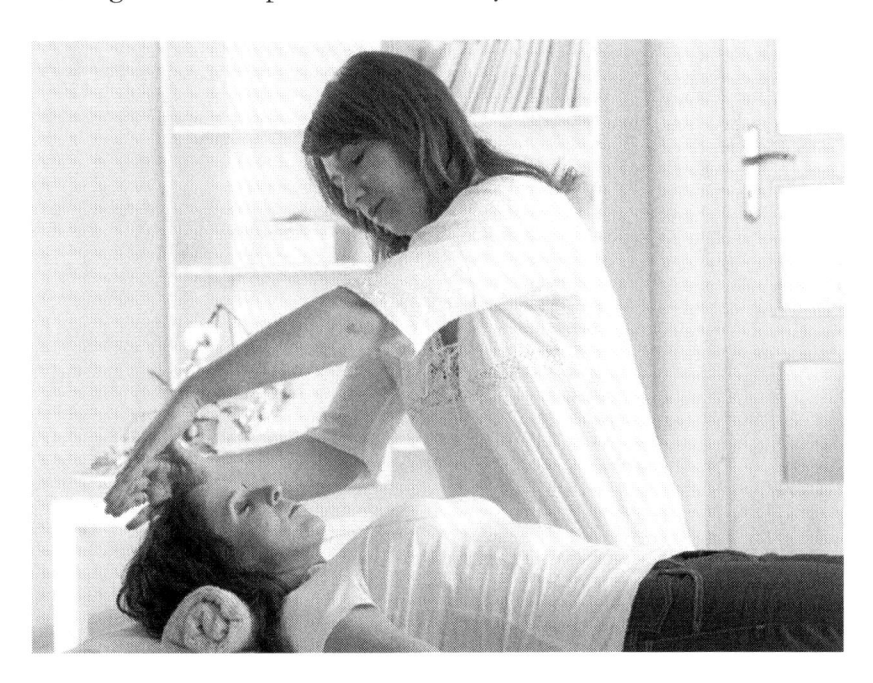

Summary

1. Gassho (informal) - palms in prayer position in front of heart center and head lowered. You can do this in your mind or physically at the start of a session or meditation.
2. Reiji-Ho - you will draw Reiki in through you and use the symbols to help you clear yourself in preparation for the session. You can raise your hands to your third eye and set the intention that the client/recipient will draw in Reiki energy to help them clear any imbalances. You will ask to receive guidance during the session and trust that your hands will go where needed.
3. Chiryo - you can then move to the client's crown chakra and place your dominant hand over the area. When you feel called to move to the next position you will do so and conduct the session.

Essentially it is clearing, setting an intention and then releasing expectations, the desire to control and focus on witnessing the session.

Breath

The body and consciousness are connected by breath. Breath work can be used to access different levels of consciousness. We breathe in oxygen for physical survival, and universal life force to nourish and cleanse our spirit. Dr. Usui taught his students a breathing technique called Joshin Kokyuu-Ho which translates as "breathing to cleanse the spirit".

Joshin Kokyuu-Ho

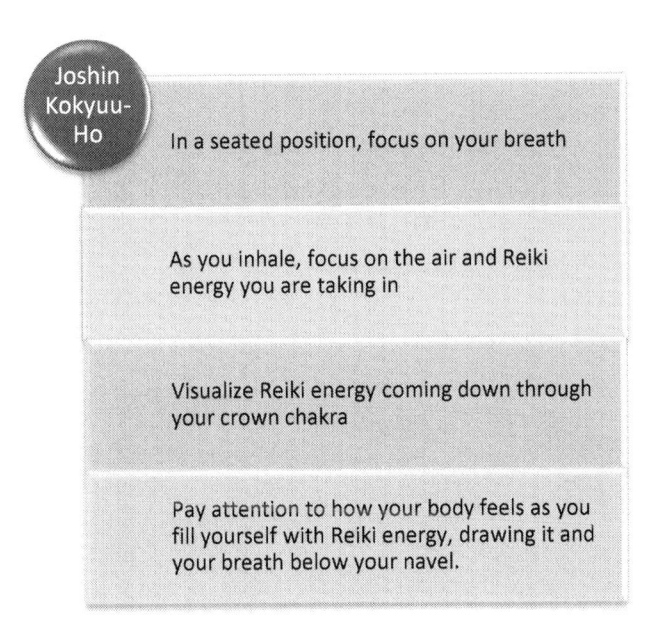

- In a seated position, focus on your breath
- As you inhale, focus on the air and Reiki energy you are taking in
- Visualize Reiki energy coming down through your crown chakra
- Pay attention to how your body feels as you fill yourself with Reiki energy, drawing it and your breath below your navel.

The Dan Tian

The Dan Tian is located in the abdomen between the navel and pubic bone. The Dan Tian holds a reservoir of energy. By taking time to connect with this energy point, you can increase your vitality and ensure you are a clear channel for Reiki energy.

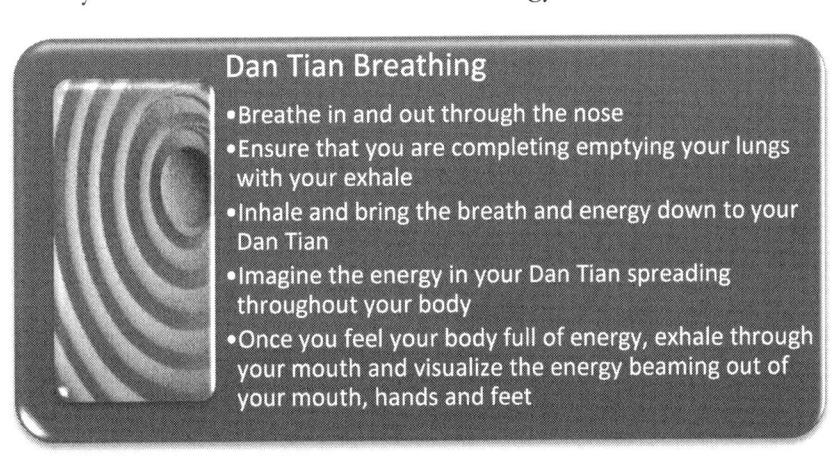

Dan Tian Breathing

- Breathe in and out through the nose
- Ensure that you are completing emptying your lungs with your exhale
- Inhale and bring the breath and energy down to your Dan Tian
- Imagine the energy in your Dan Tian spreading throughout your body
- Once you feel your body full of energy, exhale through your mouth and visualize the energy beaming out of your mouth, hands and feet

Distance Reiki

The three Usui Reiki symbols combined allow the practitioner to perform distance healing.

You will want to practice drawing the symbols until you can visualize all three of them clearly without referring to your notes. Drawing the symbols can be a very effective form of meditation. You may also find intoning the symbols as you draw them to be a meaningful practice.

There are many ways to use and channel Reiki through the symbols. As you work with the symbols you will find the method that works best. For example, some people prefer to draw them in the air with their hands, others draw them on the roof of their mouth with their tongue. Some visualize them with their mind.

With practice you will be able to perform Reiki with recipient short and long distances from you.

When you begin to practice distance Reiki, follow the guidelines below.

1. Find a quiet place and ensure you have enough time to not be interrupted.
2. Decide which distance method you are going to use to channel Reiki before you begin the session (methods outlined below – example, surrogate, paper etc.)

3. Ground yourself and connect with Reiki. This can be done by drawing Reiki energy in and running it through your feet and into the ground.
4. Clear your mind and release any expectations regarding the session. Remember that you are the channel for Reiki and you will witness Reiki, which will do the work and will be travelling across time and space to connect with the recipient of the session.
5. Once you feel you are connected with Reiki, allow Reiki energy to flow using the method you have decided upon. Remember that all methods are effective, so you will want to try them all so that you can decide on your favourite method(s) to use in the future.
6. Continue the distance session for as long as you intuitively feel it should continue. Reiki will go where it is needed and continue to work even after you have ended the session. The key with distance sessions is intention.
7. After the distance healing session, release the outcome to the wisdom and love of Reiki. Trust that Reiki will be a part of the best possible outcome for the recipient.
8. Set the intention that the session is over. You may also find it helpful to wash your hands under cold running water and or to drink a glass of cold water.

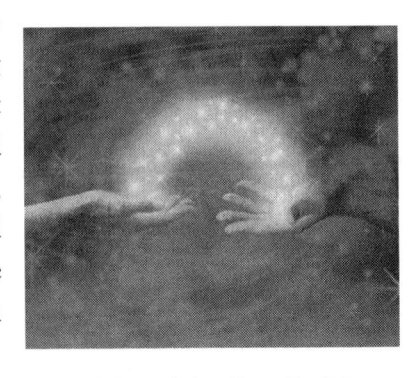

Ways to Perform Distance Reiki

Just as when you perform in person sessions, it is helpful to have a routine in place so you can feel relaxed and focused on the energy rather than the physical aspects of the session.

Just like learning to ride a bike, in the beginning it can feel overwhelming to think about all of the things you need to do and pay attention to in order to keep from falling over. With repetition and practice, the combination of actions will be imprinted in your subconscious mind and you can then enjoy the experience.

Similarly, once you have mastered performing a distance Reiki session, you will be able to relax and enjoy on the session. As your confidence in your practice grows, you will find your intuition speaks more strongly.

You will need to choose a way to visualize what is happening during the session because in distance work, the recipient will not be in front of you. Below are some ways to help you visualize the recipient in your mind's eye.

When you are setting the intention at the beginning of the distance session, remember that you do not have any control regarding the outcome of the session, nor what is in the best interests of the recipient. You must remove your ego and its desires and allow Reiki with its infinite wisdom to do what is needed based on the recipient's best interests – not your perception of what is best for them.

This intention keeps the responsibility of healing with Reiki energy to do what is needed and go where it is needed. In some cases, the results of a session may not be as your recipient would like them to be. This can be frustrating especially if the person you want to receive healing is a family member or friend, but you must respect that the recipient draws in the Reiki energy that is needed and Reiki will work in the best interests of the recipient.

The Surrogate Method

There are a variety of things you can use as a surrogate in a Reiki session. The most important thing you must do is at the beginning of the distance session is to set the intention that the surrogate is representing the person, animal, thing or situation you are sending Reiki to. A photograph, stuffed animal, pen, crystal or the details of the recipient written on a piece of paper are some examples of an effective surrogate.

Many Reiki practitioners have a favourite surrogate such as a stuffed animal and use it for all of their distance sessions. When performing distance Reiki sessions with people using a surrogate you may find that you prefer to use an item such as teddy bear as you are able to work more precisely. For example, if a person has an injured right arm, you can spend more time treating the surrogate teddy bears right arm.

Another method is as follows. For example, you want to channel Reiki to your friend who is sick, has asked for a Reiki session and is in another country. First you will find a photograph of your friend. Then you will write down her name, and the location she is in. Choose a time when you both will be able to relax and won't be disturbed. Place the photo and the piece of paper in your hands. If no one is able to see or hear you, you can set your intention out loud adding that the photo will be used as a surrogate for your friend.

You will then visualize your friend lying down. Holding the photo and piece of paper in your non-dominant hand draw the Reiki sandwich over the top with your dominant hand. You will intone the symbols and hold the intention that the Reiki session will be for your friend's highest good. Then, fold your hands together and imagine sending healing light to your friend for as long as you feel called to.

Once you have performed the session, take a moment to gives thanks to Reiki energy.

In your sessions, you need to remember that the recipient is drawing in the Reiki energy and doing the healing, you are the conduit. The recipient needs to be open and ready to work with you to help them on their healing journey.

You can also program the symbols by setting the intention that the Reiki energy is channelled for a specific amount of time over a number of days. You will want the recipient to take the time each day to tune into receiving the Reiki energy.

Using your body as a Surrogate

Another way you can perform distance sessions is by using your own body to represent the body of the recipient. You can perform the hand positions for a complete self-treatment with the understanding that your body is a surrogate for the recipient's body.

Another method is to use a part of your body such as your legs to represent the recipient. It is easiest to do this while seated. You will use one of your knees and thighs to represent the head and front of their body (for example, the left). Your knee represents the recipient's head, the middle of your thigh is the recipient's body and the top portion of your thigh as it meets your hip is the recipient's legs and feet. The other knee and thigh will represent the back of the recipient's head and body.

This type of session takes less time to complete than a traditional session. By using your left hand to perform Reiki with your left knee and thigh and your right hand for your right knee and thigh, you can complete the session with three positions lasting approximately five minutes per position. You may also want to draw or visualize Reiki symbols when you feel called to. You will then close the session with gratitude for Reiki energy and sweep the recipient's aura by gently sweeping your hands above your knees and thighs.

Visualizing during Distance Reiki

There are many ways you can visualize and receive information during your distance Reiki sessions. Here are some examples. You can see which feels right for you.

First you will want to close your eyes and set your intention. You will repeat the recipient's name three times to focus your mind and establish an energetic connection between yourself and the recipient. Now in your mind's eye, see the recipient in a miniature form relaxing in the palms of your hands. With that image in mind, open your eyes and beam the Reiki symbols from your third eye chakra onto the recipient you are visualizing.

Now you will gently cup your hands together and keep them closed for as long as you intuitively feel is needed. When you feel the session is complete, close your eyes and set the intention that you are transporting the recipient back to their home or place they are currently residing. You can also set the intention that their body will continue to use Reiki energy for as long as needed. You will close the session with gratitude for Reiki and wash your hands in cold running water once you are finished to help your body ground.

Another way to visualize during a distance Reiki session is to travel to where the recipient is located in your mind's eye. You would close your eyes and visualize the recipient and then set the intention that you will be performing Reiki for the highest good of the recipient. Then visualize the recipient lying down. You will then perform a complete self-treatment in your mind's eye on the recipient.

When you are finished, you will send gratitude to Reiki energy and close the session, with the intention that you return home. You will then use your preferred grounding techniques.

Creating Your Mental Reiki Room

Just as you have a physical place where you meditate and perform Reiki on yourself and others, it can be very helpful to have a mental space where you can perform Reiki and find peace. The meditation steps below will help you to create a Reiki space in your mind's eye that you can effectively use to conduct Reiki sessions, meditate and connect with your intuition. You can read through the steps and then complete them on your own or if you have access to the course, please visit this guided meditation there now.

Try to find a space where you can move freely to complete this meditation. Begin seated or lying down.

Close your eyes

Take a few deep breaths focusing on feeling the air enter your body and fill your chest

Pause

Feel your toes relax and allow that relaxation to spread through your feet.

Concentrate on your calves, feel them release.

Remember to breathe

Your thighs relax and that wave spreads up through your torso.

With your exhale, your chest and back release. The calm spreads down through your arms and hands.

Focus on your breathing – in and out

Your neck relaxes and the muscles in your face and head release

All is well

Now imagine that you are outside surrounded by nature

This place is one where you feel at ease. It may be by water, or in a field of flowers. It might be in a forest or a meadow. You feel at peace here.

Now focus on your root chakra at the base of your spine. See the energy spinning like a fan, emanating the deep colour of red.

Take a few deep breaths.

Move your focus up to your sacral chakra, located just below your navel. Watch as the orange ball of energy swirls.

Take a moment and just breathe.

Shift your focus up to your solar plexus chakra. Feel the yellow energy moving and turning around and around.

Breathe.

Now focus on your heart chakra. Breathe into the green circle of energy allowing it to expand.

Continue to breathe into your heart centre.

Pay attention to your throat chakra. Watch the shades of blue spin.

Take a few moments to just be.

Move your focus to your third-eye chakra. Feel the purple energy emanating through the front and back of your head.

Breathe and allow that energy to circle.

Focus on your crown chakra. Watch as the ball of purple white light shines and emanates a bright pure light.

Breathe.

Your attention is guided back to your surroundings.

You notice there is a path and you begin walking it.

The path meanders and you are lead to some steps. You climb them, one, two, three, four, five and you arrive at a clearing.

This is where you will build your Reiki healing room.

Decide on what the building will look like and what it will be made of. Any materials are at your disposal.

It could be a one room log cabin or a tent.

It could be a 6-bedroom home with a swimming pool.

It could be made of bricks and resemble a clinic.

The choice is yours. Allow your intuition to guide you.

The materials will appear as you need them.

Begin building. You may find it helpful to open your eyes, get up out of your position and find some space and go through the motions of building your space. (Make sure your physical surroundings give you the space to move and be safe if you close your eyes again)

You build the outer walls of your Reiki space. You may have windows or not. You create your door that only you will enter through. This door will be hidden and not accessible by anyone but you.

Now you will create your door for clients. This can be an ornate ancient carved door or it may be a modern glass door with electronic access. Again the choice is yours.

Here you will install a light that shines down on your door and your clients or those you invite into your Reiki space.

This light will serve as a gatekeeper and will only allow those who will benefit from being in your Reiki space as well as keep any energy/individuals out who would not serve your highest good.

You will set that light to shine bright on those you welcome to your space. It will also help individuals release any thoughts/memories/energy that is no longer serving their highest good.

You enter your Reiki space. Look around. Envision how this space will serve you and the good work you will do on yourself and with others.

Begin putting up the walls of your rooms, painting them, adding decorations. You may want a treatment table in your Reiki room. You may want a couch in your lounge area for talking with clients and individuals you invite into your healing area.

You may find that additional rooms make themselves known such as an exercise room or an office or a place you can mediate.

Put the finishing touches on your space. Now sit in your Reiki space and intend that the power and wisdom of Reiki permeate this space and those who enter it.

This will be a place for you to find peace and clarity. You may find this is an effective space for you to hold distance Reiki sessions.

This is also a space where you can invite those individuals in with whom you need to find balance and resolution. You may also find this space a place where you can find guidance.

In order to enter this space from now on, you can first imagine you are surrounded by nature. Then you will meditate on your chakras as we did earlier. Then you will follow the path and steps to your space.

You can spend as much time in this space as you choose and may find that your intuition connects strongly with you there.

When you are ready to leave you leave through your door.

This space that you have created may change over time, but it will always be there for you.

How to Perform a Distance Reiki Session

Permission

When you are conducting a Reiki session with someone in person, the recipient provides clear consent by coming to you. When performing a distance Reiki session, you need to ensure that you have the recipient's permission to perform Reiki in order to work within legal parameters, maintain an ethical practice and integrity as a practitioner.

Although in your judgement you may feel that the recipient is in dire need of a Reiki session, they need to make the conscious choice to participate in their healing with Reiki. There are always individuals who will benefit from your work and be eager and willing participants.

Generally, a person in need of Reiki will contact you for a session. This request for a session (either in-person of from a distance) gives you permission to conduct a Reiki session.

In some cases, you will receive a request for distance Reiki for another person. If you aren't sure that you have the person's consent, you can choose to do one of the following.

If you have decided never to send Reiki to anyone unless they request it personally you can simply refuse to conduct a Reiki session (this is recommended when working with other Reiki practitioners as they will have no difficulties asking for a session when they need one).

Another option is to perform Reiki on the person who is requesting Reiki for another. By doing this, both the person asking and the person in need can benefit as Reiki will go where it is needed.

The third option is to connect with the person intuitively and ask for their consent on an energetic level. This can be helpful in cases where a person cannot communicate physically. You can do this by meditating, and creating a picture in your mind of the person with whom you want to connect. In your mind's eye, ask them the question: "Would you like to receive Reiki with the intention of healing on all levels?" If you get a clear yes or no, then proceed accordingly.

In the case of an emergency, if you are asked to perform Reiki for someone who is unable to ask for themselves, you can perform the session with the intention that the session be for the highest good of all concerned. You will want to ensure that before you do so you are not contravening any laws in your area.

In these cases, you will want to hold the understanding that Reiki will go where it is needed and only where it is desired. In this way, if an individual is not ready to heal in a specific area, Reiki will focus on the areas they are ready to balance.

Most practitioners develop a preference of what feels best for them regarding permission. Be open to your beliefs shifting with time and experience.

If you find that you often want to channel Reiki to those who do not wish to receive it, the person you need to work with is yourself. Make sure you keep up your daily self-treatments and set the intention that you are ready to heal any imbalances related to you wanting to perform Reiki on those who are not ready to receive it.

Steps to Performing a Distance Reiki Session

The guidelines are a starting point. You can try other methods as you feel called to and can choose the process that feels best for you at that time. There is no single correct way to perform a session. The steps below are similar to what Dr. Usui called Enkaku Chiryo.

1. Receive permission to perform the session
2. Hold the photo of the recipient and visualize the symbols on top of the photo while intoning their names.
   - Cho Ku Rei (Power symbol)
   - Sei He Ki (Mental/Emotional symbol)
   - Cho Ku Rei (Power symbol)
   - Hon Sha Ze Sho Nen (Distance symbol)
   - Cho Ku Rei (Power symbol)
3. Focus on the recipient and cup your hands around the photo.
4. In your mind's eye, imagine that you are with the recipient and they are ready to begin the session.
5. Mentally draw the symbols over the recipient, intoning the names of the symbols three times.
6. Perform a complete Reiki session. As you perform each positon, pay attention to the sensations you receive and stay where you feel your hands need to.

7. Once you feel the session is ready to end, you can close the session as you normally would. You will want to set the intention that the session is over and send thanks to Reiki.

8. With the session being over, you will want to ground yourself by washing your hands in cold water and drinking a glass of cold water.

Remember this is only a guide. You will come across many different Reiki practitioners and master/teachers that will offer variations on every Reiki technique.

Distance Reiki Possibilities

In your Reiki practice, you may already be noticing that when you think about Reiki or are around others who may be ready to receive Reiki, it begins to flow. This can feel like heat or cold in our hands and body.

As mentioned earlier, the Hon Sha Ze Sho Zen symbol can not only help bridge space in the distance work we do but also time.

With this symbol you can also perform Reiki with the past, present or future.

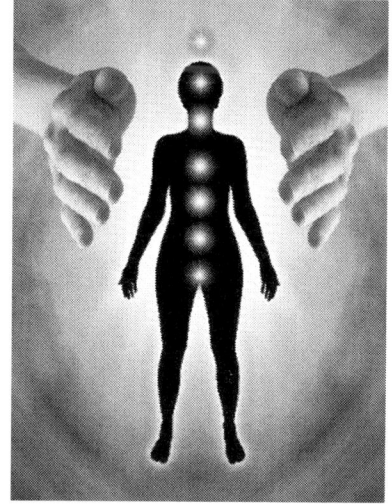

Performing Reiki Across Time

So far, we have explored how Reiki can be used to work with individuals across short or long distances. When you are performing distance Reiki, you can set the time that the session is received. An example would be if you live in the United States and you want to perform a session with someone in Australia who is going into surgery the following morning at 10 a.m. (Australian Local Time). The time difference may make performing the session at the time of the surgery very inconvenient. A solution is to perform the session at the time that is convenient for you and at the beginning of the session, set the intention that Reiki will be drawn in by the recipient in preparation for the surgery. The body of the recipient will then draw in Reiki at the time that is best to help prepare for the procedure.

Performing Reiki with the Future

Just as there are times when you will be unable to perform a session at the exact time the recipient would like to receive it, there are also occasions that you or a recipient will want to prepare for. These can include things such as interviews, exams, meetings, weddings, surgeries, giving birth etc. These sessions can be performed with the intent of helping the bodymind of the recipient prepare for these important instances.

In these sessions, you will set the intention that the body draw in the Reiki energy it needs to balance in preparation for the event.

Performing Reiki with the Past

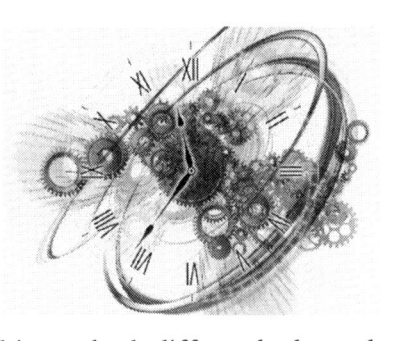

When an event occurs that triggers strong emotions, the bodymind has a choice. It can choose to process the emotions in the moment and allow them to pass through. This enables us to discern the wisdom we are meant to take from the event. The second choice is to resist the event and emotions. This can look differently depending on the situation and individual. The resistance usually ends up with the emotions being stored in the bodymind and the beliefs connected to the event fortified. Over time, these beliefs and emotions can cause not only energetic imbalances but physical as well. Performing a Reiki session with the intention of balancing past events can help the recipient to process the emotions and beliefs connected to that event so that any physical imbalances connected with them can heal as they were intended to. This can be helpful in so many instances. Events such as accidents can be focused on or you can extend the period to include a span of time such as fetal life. Although the session will not alter the history of the individual, it will help them to release energy so they do not continue to suffer.

Past Lives and Reiki

At birth, to some extent we already have stored behavioural traits, attitudes, fears, illnesses and beliefs from our parents, ancestors, religions and memories. These inherited traits can cause imbalances that affect our lives. A person for example may have had a paralyzing fear of fire from a very young age or another individual could have numerous unexplained symptoms that will not resolve. In these cases, inherited memory could be the trigger.

Modern science has only decoded a very small portion of our genetic code (ex: 5 inches of a six-foot strand), and it is thought that this information is likely stored somewhere along the strand. Regardless of location, Reiki can effectively work to balance this information.

In these cases, the memories are not your "past life" experiences. Rather, they are cellular memories and traits that have been passed on from previous generations (not necessarily within your blood line). Like your eye color, and instinctual traits that keep you alive you also have inherent beliefs and tendencies imprinted on your genetic code. For the most part, the genetic code is not fixed and can be modified.

Reiki can help to balance what is occurring between the bodymind at this time and the many influences from the past that are affecting it. This can include physical traits or hereditary illnesses passed on, cultural behaviour patterns, inherited religious dogma or fears, past traumas, major events, disasters, and environmental factors from man-made things such as genetically modified foods and pollution.

In some cases, these traits or tendencies can be connected to an imbalance at a physical level. In others, these past influences can be influencing mental, emotional and energetic aspects.

Reiki can help to balance the hereditary trait in connection to the bodymind so that the information can be processed and utilized constructively when needed, and no longer has an unconscious effect on the individual.

The Sei He Ki symbol can be used to help address these triggers. Some practitioners find working at the crown chakra and using the mental emotional symbol or the master symbol (once you are attuned and familiar with it) to focus the Reiki energy very powerful.

You may find during a session you receive images or memories from a time past. It is helpful to know that this is likely an inherited memory that is ready to be balanced.

If you do receive such information during a session, try to be general when discussing this with your client. Hearing that there was a memory of being burned in Salem is not something someone may want to hear and they may attach to it which will have an effect on the clearing of it. Broad statements such as "we were working with some residual fears around being judged" are preferred.

Remember that Reiki will go where needed, when it is needed and no additional techniques are required to do this powerful work.

Transcending Time and Space in Self-Treatments

Just as you can use the Hon Sha Ze Sho Nen symbol to bridge time and space with others. You can also benefit from sessions with this intent.

In the sessions you perform of yourself, you can focus on any past event or situations where you experienced pain or trauma. Doing so can not only bring relief but also help you to see the bigger picture of your life. Rather than carrying the emotions and beliefs that do not resonate, you will be able to release them so you are more present and clear. If you find yourself getting emotional when you are performing Reiki on past events, allow the emotions to rise and be released with love. They have served their purpose and are no longer needed.

When you are feeling tired and are resisting the present moment, try centering yourself for a few minutes and focus on your breath. Then draw in Reiki energy through your crown chakra until you are full and beaming Reiki. Continue to focus on your breath and with each breath, feel the energy move with it.

You can also perform sessions on yourself with a focus on your future self and life. Your focus can be on a specific event or time and can be a week or years from now. As you perform these sessions, consider how you would like to feel in that future moment. That feeling is a frequency. Now allow Reiki to amplify that frequency and strengthen it. The more time you spend with that resonance, the more you will attract it in the present and future.

Reiki in the World

As you know, the possible applications of Reiki are limitless. Here are some additional ways Reiki can be used.

We exist because the earth allows us to. In gratitude for the food and sustenance we receive, we can perform Reiki with our earth. You can focus on a specific location that may be in need or the planet in general.

When you become aware of an accident, you can allow it to draw Reiki energy in for the highest good of all concerned.

In places of conflict, you can allow the situation including the land the conflict is on to draw Reiki energy in for the highest good of all concerned.

In times and places where an attack has occurred, remain in a heart centered space and allow the place and situation to drawn in Reiki energy.

When global events are occurring such as political meetings or elections, you can allow Reiki to be drawn in by the event for the highest good of all.

In the examples provided, you would perform a distance session as you normally do. In these cases, you will not be asking for permission from the individuals involved so your focus will be on the situation and location and if there are individuals who would like to receive Reiki, they will draw it in as needed.

Working with Groups

As your practice evolves, your schedule will as well. You can perform Reiki on more than one person at a time if needed. One way to do so is by using a Reiki box.

Write down the names of the people or situations that will receive Reiki. You can also include photographs if you have them. You will place your hands above or beside the box and allow the recipients to draw in the energy. If you do not have a box, a bowl or envelope can be used. Keep that item reserved for Reiki sessions to help maintain focus.

You can perform Reiki with the box each day and adjust the recipients as needed.

If you enjoy working with crystals, you could create a crystal grid and charge it with Reiki energy just as you would with your Reiki box. You could select crystals and create a layout specific to the focus you are working with.

Another way to work with groups of individuals or situations is to use a vision board. In this case you would have a space where you posted the photos of the people and their information as well as any situations that you were working with in one common place and spend time performing Reiki with the board.

Using Reiki with Your Goals

You can also use your Reiki box to help you manifest your goals and dreams. Here are some steps to do so.

Step 1: Create Your Ideal Life on Paper

Write out what your ideal day at work and at play looks like. From the moment you get up until the moment you go to sleep, describe everything from what surrounds you to the people you spend time with.

Step 2: Find the Feelings

Now, review your idea life. There are actions and objects and people in it, but what you want to focus on is how you want to feel throughout those days. Do you want to feel free, loving, wealthy and inspired? Do you want to feel powerful, healthy, lean and joyful? Do you want to feel supported, connected, happy and healthy? Write out the feelings.

Step 3: Feel the Vibration

Take some time and look at each feeling. Take the feeling into your body and allow each cell to resonate that feeling. Breathe energy into that feeling until you feel it infusing your body completely. Sit with that vibration. Do that with each feeling you have identified.

Step 4: Write Your Feelings Out On Separate Small Pieces of Paper

Write each feeling out on a small piece of paper that will fit nicely into your Reiki box.

Step 5: Hold Each Feeling and Resonate

One by one, hold each piece of paper and feel that feeling. Once you have soaked your entire being in that feeling, place the paper in the Reiki box. Then take the next piece of paper and feel that feeling. Place it in your Reiki box.

Step 6: Beam Reiki to Your Reiki Box

Now that all of your feelings/desires are in your Reiki box, release them and clear your mind. Ground yourself as you normally would before a Reiki session and set the intention that your desired feelings will draw in the Reiki energy they need to help you manifest your ideal life. Once the intention is set, clear your mind and allow Reiki to be drawn through you to your Reiki box. Your session can last as long as you feel it needs to.

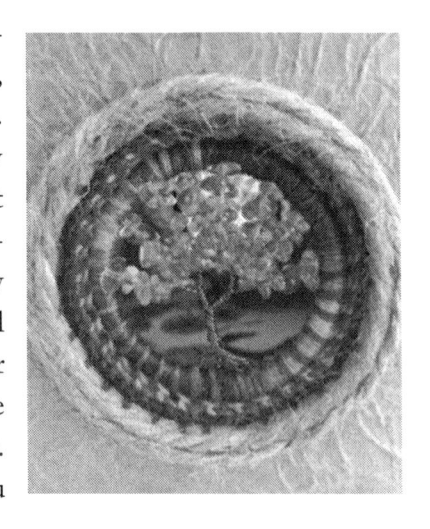

Each day, ideally first thing in the morning as soon as you wake up take out each feeling/piece of paper and perform steps 5 and 6.

By letting Reiki energy infuse your desired feelings, you will be increasing your resonance with those feelings and like a magnet will transform your world to align with those feelings.

Another technique you can use when manifesting your goals is to write out your specific goals on a piece of paper and then draw the Reiki symbols on top of the goal. You can then allow the goal to draw in Reiki. Keep that paper close to you and perform Reiki with it each day. You will set the intention that it be for the highest good of all concerned and then release your expectations. The wisdom of Reiki will handle the rest.

Problem-Solving with Reiki

When you have an imbalance in your body or life, how do you usually handle it?

Most of us will seek external solutions, whether it is adding a new supplement to our diet or changing jobs. Although there is nothing wrong with taking action and many times these actions lead to other positive changes, you need to consider the progression imbalance takes in our lives.

Before any invention is created, it starts off as an idea. Where that idea comes from is still not scientifically validated so for now we will call it the collective. So, an inventor pulls an idea from the collective. She then creates a design, blueprint or prototype and hires the necessary people to construct the invention. At the end of this progression a physical product is made that reflects the initial idea.

We tend to approach problems at the product level rather than the thought that conceived it. Remember that the product reflects the idea. Our bodies are constantly replicating. You have a new heart every 20 years, new lungs every 2-3 weeks and new taste buds every 10 days. Why is it that a body part regenerates itself in a flawed condition? It is because the cells are creating a product that is a reflection of the idea (in our bodies case, a morphogenic field). Rather than focusing on fixing the knee (which of course can be necessary), a focus on balancing the blueprint of the knee will ensure that the actual product (physical knee) is balanced as a result.

TOP-DOWN Cause & Effect

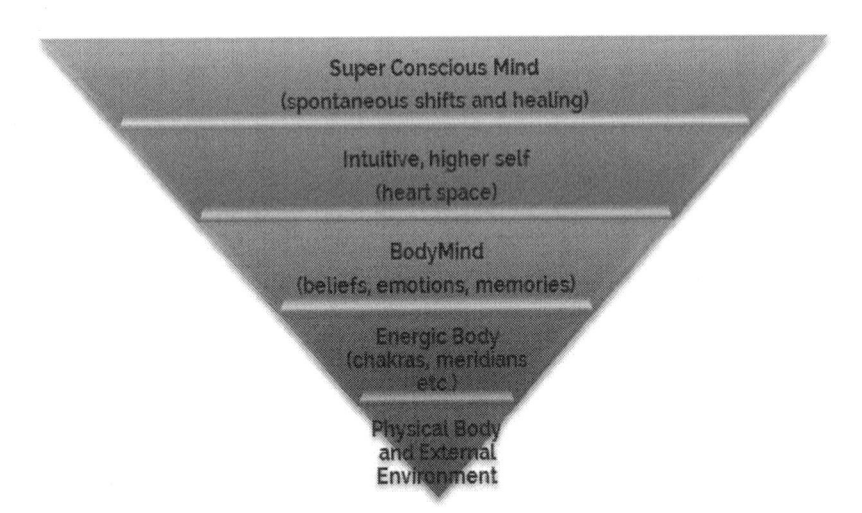

Super Conscious Mind
(spontaneous shifts and healing)

Intuitive, higher self
(heart space)

BodyMind
(beliefs, emotions, memories)

Energic Body
(chakras, meridians etc.)

Physical Body
and External
Environment

The positive thing to remember is that with Reiki and some other alternative modalities, you are working at the level of the intuitive, higher self. Your focus is not on diagnosing or finding a solution, rather it is to be in balance and allow Reiki energy to flow where it is needed.

List three things you would like to see change in. It can be a physical aspect of your body, a belief system that is no longer serving you or an aspect of your life you are dis-satisfied with. Take 10 minutes, and perform a Reiki session on yourself with the intent that one item on your list is addressed. After 10 minutes, move on to your second item and perform Reiki on yourself with the focus on that item. Then perform a Reiki session on the third item on your list. Make notes on any thoughts or feelings that came to mind during your sessions.

If you make a habit of addressing imbalances this way in addition to any external actions you take, you may be pleasantly surprised at the shifts your body, mind and life experience.

Preparing To Work with Clients

Before you perform Reiki sessions on others, it is ideal to clear the space you are working in. You can do so by using the Reiki symbols. You may feel called to use only the Cho Ku Rei symbol with the intention of releasing negative energy, or you may use additional symbols such as the Sei He Ki with a focus of releasing mental/emotional energy.

It is also helpful to ensure you are clear and ready to work with another. This can be done by taking a few deep breaths and drawing Reiki in. You can use the symbols to release any energy within that is not serving you and when you feel full with Reiki energy you can begin.

At the start of the session you can mentally draw or beam the symbols on to your hands and above the recipient's body. You can then be open to observing the symbols entering the recipient's body with each hand position. Remember to release your expectations regarding how the session should look and feel as well as the outcome. Remember that their body knows best and the session intention is for the highest good.

Using Tools

Although in our work with Reiki, we are in the process of unlearning and releasing the beliefs and energy that is not serving us, in some cases it can be helpful to use tools that will build positive beliefs for the recipient. Our ego needs be confident and healthy before it is ready to begin releasing unwanted energy and habits. If an individual comes to you with a specific focus such as an unwanted habit, you can use a tool to help the client focus during the session. An example of a tool is an affirmation that they would repeat to themselves. This statement needs to be framed in the positive such as "I love to eat healthy whole foods" or "I am free from smoking". The recipient will focus on how they want to feel with the new positive habit and Reiki will help to activate and amplify that energy. You can also have the client write the statement on a piece of paper and hold it throughout the session. They can then take the paper home and meditate with it each day.

Working with the Aura

Before you begin a session you can focus on the recipient's aura. As you run your hands above the recipient's body, pay attention to the sensations and information you receive. You may sense hot or cold areas or receive a message to focus on a specific area. The intention here is not to diagnose any issues, but to introduce yourself to the energy of the recipient.

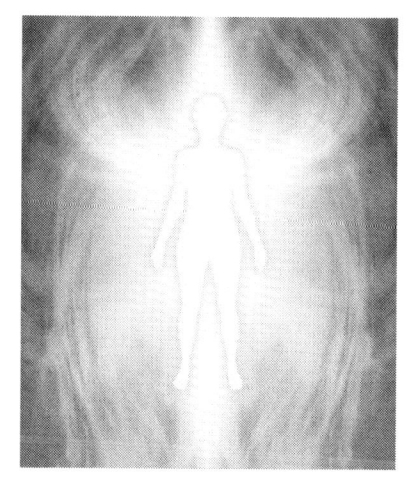

Starting Your Reiki Practice

You have learned the techniques needed to perform Reiki on others in person and from a distance. It is up to you to decide if Reiki is something you would like to pursue as a more formal practice with the public.

The benefits of being a Reiki Practitioner are that you can set your own hours. You may want to pursue this in addition to your current profession. Then as your practice builds you can decide whether you would like to pursue Reiki on a full time basis. Another benefit is that you benefit physically, mentally and emotionally from the sessions you perform with clients. Imagine having a job that improved your well-being.

As a Reiki practitioner, you are your own boss. You can set your session fees and choose the clients you wish to work with. The drawbacks as with any business are that in most cases you are also the receptionist who takes appointments, the accountant who manages the finances and the marketing rep who promotes your business. This profession can be an amazing way to make a living for the right person. Is that you?

Keep in mind that once you complete your Reiki Master Level, you have the ability to certify other Reiki practitioners and teach Reiki. This can also add to your income as well as add to your business as a practitioner. You will likely find that many of your clients eventually also become students.

If you are a licensed practitioner in another health care modality (e.g., chiropractors, physiotherapists, massage therapists, nurses etc.) you can incorporate Reiki into your sessions as soon as you are confident with the techniques.

If you are a Reiki student who comes from non-health care background, you can also start working with people as soon as you feel ready. Applying the newly learned material is the best way to become proficient and gain confidence with the techniques. You can tell clients (be they family members, friends or others) that you have just learned a new modality and are working towards your Master Level, a process which includes gathering experience from conducting a minimum of 50 sessions. As there is no risk of doing harm to the client with Reiki techniques, there is no reason to wait to practice on people who could benefit from the work. You can tell them that the techniques you have learned are powerful, and that their body is in control of the session.

You may also be wondering if you can charge for your sessions right away. In this case, the choice is yours. Health care practitioners who have learned Reiki and are incorporating it into their sessions will likely wish to continue charging for their treatments. The key is that you are confident when following the standard techniques in a session. Some students reach this level by the end of Reiki Level 2, but others want to have more practice before performing professional sessions.

The concept of having an energy exchange between the practitioner and client is important. With new practitioners, you will likely be working with friends and family who will be giving their time to help you practice. Eventually, the energy exchange may become that the recipient who has experienced positive benefits shares their enthusiasm to bring you additional clients. Then you may wish to work on a donation basis for those who have come from a referral. The speed at which you proceed through these stages will depend on you.

While you practice working with others it is so important that you keep up your daily self-treatments. Those will help you become a clear conduit for the energy and improve your practice.

As you are working through the course, it is likely you have developed the understanding that there is more to becoming a Reiki Practitioner than simply attending a couple of weekend workshops. Practice and an openness to refining your own awareness will help you to become the best practitioner you can be.

Non Traditional Reiki Symbols

The three traditional Usui symbols can be used effectively in all situations. In your traditional attunement ceremony you are attuned to those symbols which have been passed down from Dr. Usui.

Over time, some Masters found or created additional symbols that resonated with them and they began to incorporate them into their own practice and teachings. These non-traditional symbols in some cases were used to distinguish one Master and their teachings from another.

There are some Masters that believe you can only work with the non-traditional symbols if you have been specifically attuned to them. This is especially the case when referring to symbols that are a part of a trademarked system. There are however many Masters who do not hold this belief and use the non-traditional symbols effectively in their sessions when they feel called to.

The non-traditional symbols are included in this manuals and they are a part of the consciousness of the course I teach and can be used effectively. I do not specifically include them in the attunements ceremony I perform but because you are introduced to the traditional symbols, you can use the non-traditional symbols if they resonate with you.

The example I could give would be if the traditional symbols were websites, the non-traditional symbols are like pages within those websites. Once you have access to the main site, you can navigate within it to the various aspects of the site.

The non-traditional symbols were symbols that appeared to a master at a point in their study which they were not attuned to. They then included them in their teachings and modified their instruction. Just as those Masters were not first attuned to those symbols, you do not have to be.

These additional symbols are not an essential part of your practice so you will want to work with each one to get a feel for the resonance associated with it and see if you feel called to use them.

When working with the non-traditional symbols, you will use the Cho Ku Rei to activate them. You will also want to intone the name of each symbol that you are working with three times. Intonation helps to strengthen the frequency of the symbol.

Reverse Cho Ku Rei

The reverse Cho Ku Rei symbol has the spiral drawn in a clockwise direction where the traditional CKR is drawn counter clockwise. When compared, the traditional and reverse CKR are similar in appearance to the double helix found in a DNA strand.

It is thought that where the traditional CKR helps to dispel negative energy, the reverse CKR brings in positive energy. One way to experiment with both CKRs is by using the traditional CKR at the beginning of activating your symbols and then include the reverse CKR at the end. You may find it brings balance and additional power to your sessions. If the symbol resonates with you, you can use it in your practice when you feel called to.

Harth

HEART-CENTERED ACTION

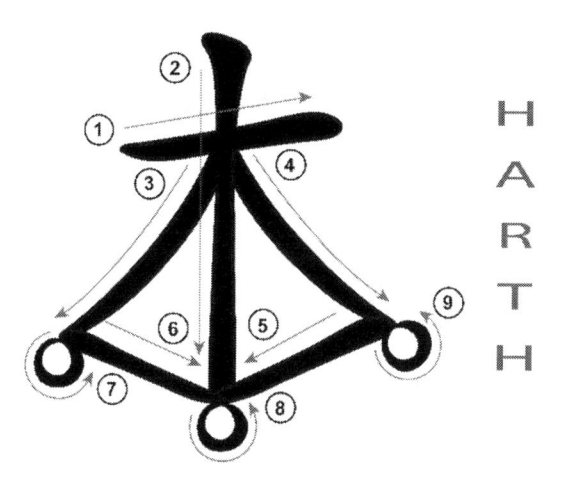

The Harth symbol is also a part of the trademarked Karuna® Reiki system. This symbol is thought to represent love, truth and harmony. The Harth symbol can be used to dissolve blocks that keep us away from the true nature of reality. Some practitioners find using the Harth symbol effective when working with addiction issue

Johre

The Johre symbol is thought to symbolize white light and can also be used to release blockages.

WHITE LIGHT

J
O
H
R
E
I

Midas Star

MIDAS STAR
OPENING UP TO RECEIVING ABUNDANCE

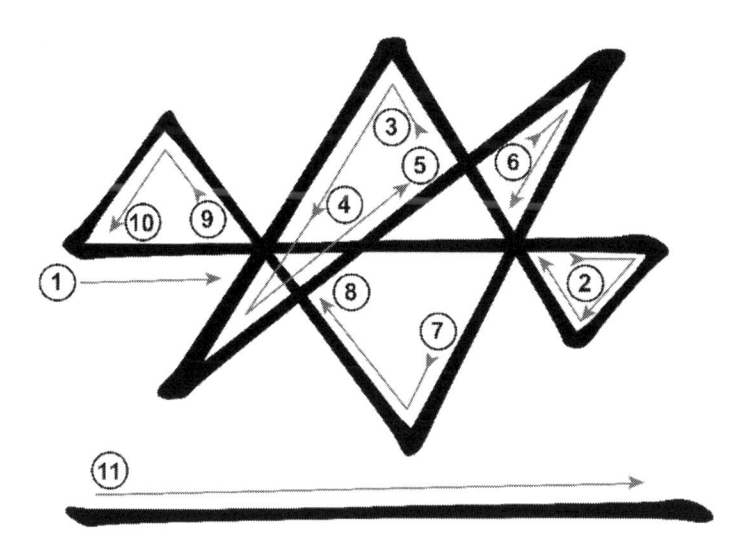

The midas star is a symbol used in Seichem Reiki and is thought to bring prosperity and success. You can try using this symbol by writing your goals on a piece of paper and then drawing the midas star symbol on top of the goals. The final line in this symbol can be drawn in the color red and is thought to add power to symbol.

Motor Zanon

MOTOR ZANON
RELEASING IMBALANCES

This symbol was originally used in Seichem Reiki and is thought to be effective when working with viruses, infection etc. Motor meaning in and zanon meaning out. This symbol can help go in and help to pull the foreign or imbalanced aspect of the body out. You may find this symbol works well with both the traditional and reverse CKR.

Raku

GROUNDING OR IGNITING ENERGY ALONG THE SPINE

R
A
K
U

This symbol is also known as the Tibetan Fire Serpent and is thought to represent the Ki energy that travels up the spine. The symbol can be drawn (as shown in the illustration above) with the direction of the stroke moving downward which will ground the energy. If it is drawn from the bottom upwards, the intention is that the energy will be drawn into the upper chakras. This symbol can be used for spinal and back problems and is said to be good for the menopause. When attuning students, you may find using this symbol helpful in closing the energetic connection between you and the student once the ceremony is complete.

Zonar

RELEASING INHERITED MEMORIES

The Zonar symbol is associated with a trademarked branch of Reiki known as Karuna® Reiki. This symbol includes within it three infinity symbols and is thought to assist in imbalances associated with inherited memory. Those memories that may not be conscious but are imbedded in our cellular memory, can be triggered by our current life circumstances and this is one symbol that can be used to balance the energy connected to those memories.

Combining Reiki with other Health Modalities

Reiki can seamlessly work with other health modalities. Because Reiki energy balances the energetic body, it can help to increase the effectiveness of modalities that focus more on the physical and emotional levels.

For example, a massage therapist who is trained in Reiki can set the intention at the start of a session that during the massage the recipient will draw in Reiki energy as needed. The therapist will then perform the massage as usual with the added benefit of both the therapist and recipient receiving a Reiki session.

If you currently practice another modality, you will want to let your clients know that you have received training in Reiki and provide a brief explanation of what Reiki is and how it works. You can then give them the option to include Reiki as a part of their regular sessions with you.

Working with Your Past, Present and Future

Your mental Reiki room can be so helpful not only during sessions but also when you want to connect with your intuition more directly. The steps below are an example of how you can access your past, present and future.

Once you have entered your mental Reiki room, find a space where you can relax. This could be like a living room with a comfortable couch, a fireplace and a television.

Look at your television screen and watch as your life appears playing out on the screen. Imagine what success feels like and see those images on your screen. Project the Reiki symbols that you feel called to use on the screen and allow that future you to draw in the energy.

Alternatively, you may wish to watch your life in the past. If you see decisions you have made or ways that you have behaved that did not reflect your highest self, allow that past you to draw in Reiki energy and use the Reiki symbols as you feel called to.

Now, from a heart centered space, see your highest-self responding in those situations. Allow the images of your life to proceed, drawing Reiki and love in.

When a Client Does Not Feel Reiki

You just performed an amazing Reiki session on a new client. In your mind's eye you saw many shifts occur during the treatment and received some clear messages about the shifts that would continue to occur for this individual.

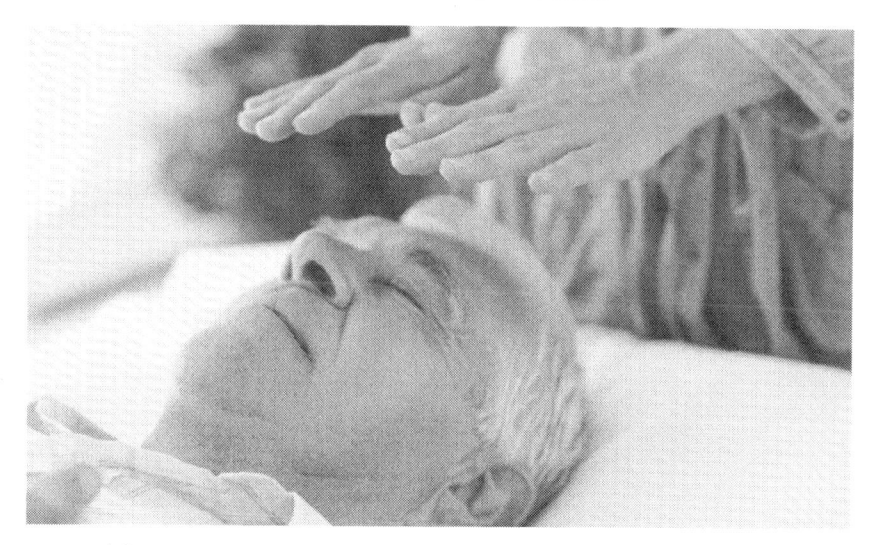

After wrapping up the session, you ask your client how they are feeling and they reply, "Fine, but I didn't feel anything during the session."

New practitioners are likely to scream inwardly, their fears as a novice being brought to light, while seasoned practitioners will likely smile a knowing smile.

Remember that shift happens and it does not need to be accompanied by bells, whistles and flashing lights to occur. Reiki energy can be very powerful and does not need to make its presence known while healing and supporting the receiver on all levels.

That being said, in order to assist your client's experience, it is a good idea to prepare them for whatever may or may not occur during a Reiki session. In your intake which should include a client history form, you may want to say:

"People sometimes notice physical sensations such as feeling tingling or changes in temperature, seeing colours, feeling light or heavy within the body, feeling sleepy, or relaxed. Others may not feel any sensations at all which is completely acceptable."

At the end of the session, you can discuss what your client experienced. This is another chance for you to reassure them that the session was effective. You will also want to alert your client to the possibility that they may find it takes their bodymind some time to process the session. Like stirring a pot of minestrone, all of the goodies rise to the surface.

When the client returns, you want to review their intake form with them by asking about the situations that brought them in for healing. For example, if the client ranked their relationship with their husband at a 9 on their intake form, you may ask, "Regarding your relationship with your husband, if a score of 10 is impossible and a score of 0 is perfect, what number would you give your relationship now?" In most cases, the client will reply with an improved number. In that case you can respond with, "Great! I am so happy that has shifted since our last session. You had given it a 9 last time." Clients usually forget when things improve (they will say-I completely forgot I had troubles with that) so this reminder is helpful in assuring them the sessions are effective.

A comprehensive intake and outtake ensures the client has clear expectations and an understanding of what the Reiki session can look like.

As the practitioner you need to trust that the session always turns out exactly as it needs to for that client. You need to remember that you are the witness of the Reiki energy and are not directing it or deciding what it heals. You need to understand that you will attract the clients that you can help the most so if they do not feel shifts during a session, that still means the session has benefited them and is in the interest of their highest good. You also need to make sure your ego is not tricking you into believing that your results need to look a certain way. You are a powerful practitioner and your work is helping to heal the world.

Animal Reiki Techniques

As you know, Reiki can be used on anything with the intention of increasing balance. Animals are very sensitive to energy and can benefit from Reiki. With the training you have completed, you can also perform Reiki with animals.

Because Reiki is non-invasive, and can do no harm, it is a wonderful way to help an animal heal. Because animals usually to have less emotional and egoic baggage, their bodies tend to be more in synch with their natural rhythms and they respond well to Reiki.

Reiki can be used with animals that are ill and in conjunction with veterinary care. Reiki can be used to help calm an animal during procedures as well as to help the body heal. Reiki can also be used to work with animals with behavioural concerns. Because poor behaviour can relate back to a trauma the animal has experienced or a belief the animal has taken on in connection with their guardian, Reiki can help to release that energy so the animal can restore their natural healthy way of being.

Communicating with Animals

Just like humans, every animal is different and will respond to you and Reiki in a different way. An animal always needs to provide their permission to receive a session before you perform Reiki. You can use your mental Reiki room to request permission or use cues from the animal's behaviour and your intuition to discern whether the animal is ready to receive Reiki.

In cases where the animal does not come close to you or acts in an aggressive manner, a distance session is always recommended. The distance can be across the room or in a completely different location.

If the animal is open to receiving Reiki and approaches you, you can gently place your hands above the animal's body. If they tolerate your touch and you are in a safe space, you can do so being gentle and paying attention to the animal's cues. If the animal moves so that your hands are in a new position, listen to that and perform Reiki on that area until they shift or you feel ready to move to the next position. If the animal shifts away from you, listen to that and continue the session from a distance.

You may find when working on guardians that their pets come to be a part of the session. You can set the intention that the pet will draw in the Reiki it needs to balance as well as the guardian.

Remember that your safety needs to be the top priority so always ensure you are in a safe space. You may want to explore training in animal care and safety if you plan to work with animals of all sizes on a regular basis.

Preparing to Perform an Animal Reiki Session

You will center and ground yourself just as you would in a typical Reiki session. You will ask for permission. If you are performing a hands on session, you can start at the head of the animal and slowly and gently work your way down.

If the animal is reluctant and does not allow you to approach it, you can perform a distance session by holding your hands toward the animal and allowing them to draw the energy in. Remember to set the intention that the session is for the highest good of all concerned.

Animals and their guardians are closely connected. In some cases, an animal may be carrying some imbalances as a way to help their guardian. In these cases, the animal may not give you permission, and you may intuitively be aware that the guardian could benefit from a session. In these cases, you can ask the guardian if they would be open to being a surrogate for the animal and you will set the intention that any imbalances that the guardian and animal share be healed.

Reiki can also be used with animals as a way to help them transition peacefully. Performing Reiki can assist with the pain a dying animal may be experiencing as well as help them to be calm. Reiki can also be used with their guardians to help process the grief they are experiencing as they release their treasured family member.

Reiki Level II Conclusion

Congratulations! You have reached the end of Level II. In this manual you have explored a variety of ways that Reiki can help you enrich your life as well as the lives of others. The possibilities are endless.

Regardless of whether you decide to continue your Reiki practice on a personal or professional level, please continue to perform Reiki on yourself each day. Even 10 minutes in the morning and evening will have such a positive difference.

When you feel called to do so, you can move on to the Master Level where you will learn how to attune others and share this wonderful gift.

Reiki III Manual

Master Degree Guide to Traditional Usui Reiki

Master Level Introduction

Congratulations on beginning your study in the Master Level. To help you learn and understand the material, the lessons have been kept concise and simple. This guide is meant to help you begin your journey with Reiki in the hopes that you will continue to learn and practice.

In this course, you will learn about the master symbol and how to use it. You will also learn how to attune others so that you can teach Reiki to others and share this amazing gift.

Once you are a Reiki Master, your adventure with Reiki is just beginning. As a Reiki Master, you will continue to learn and raise your level awareness. You can continue to help this gift spread by striving to live the 5 principles of Reiki.

The more individuals in the world that teach Reiki, the more people will benefit from this tool for healing and enlightenment. Reiki can help to raise our consciousness and heal the mentality of lack and conflict that plague our world.

In the past, to become a Reiki Master would cost thousands of dollars. A shift has occurred which allows any individual who is interested to be able to access this gift that is our birth right.

The desire to continue to grow and evolve as a loving and kind person, as well as help others are the only pre-requisites to becoming a Usui Reiki Master/Teacher.

Reiki and Symbology

Humans have used symbols as a way of communicating and transmitting power for over three hundred and fifty thousand years. Even some primates can communicate using symbols. Symbols can be categorized according to how they convey their information.

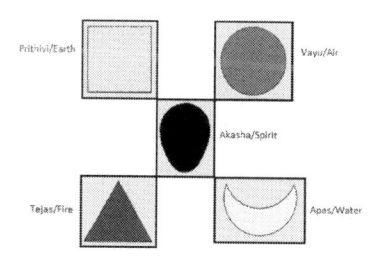

Sacred geometry or tattwas are examples of one group of symbols. Their power lies in their form.

Tattwas and in some ways Mandalas are tools that can help one to ground themselves and achieve a specific state of consciousness. Studying and drawing the symbol can stimulate the subconscious mind and energetic body. These symbols are also said to transmit information.

Another category of symbols and objects operate under the notion that they can be charged through intention, ritual or proximity to holy places or people to produce specific results. Examples of these objects include prayer beads or a rosary.

The final group of symbols are those thought to help you to connect with energy and harness its power. The symbol itself does not possess any power of its own but is used to access power. Most of the symbols used in Reiki are Kanji (written words which have symbolic meaning).

The Reiki symbols could be considered a part of the first and third group. Because they have been used for so long by so many individuals with a similar intention, the act of drawing them can elicit certain levels of consciousness as well as facilitate a connection to refined aspects of Reiki energy. The symbols do not hold power but the intention behind them does. That collective intention creates a resonance. You will likely notice that each symbol feels a little different than the other when you draw them. This is the difference in frequency. You will find that there are many different ways to draw a particular Reiki symbol, but they are all equally effective in connecting with Reiki. Instead of concerning yourself with the most effective variation of a symbol, it is better to focus on the intention and purpose of the symbol.

The Reiki symbols represent aspects of healing and enlightenment. When someone who has received the Reiki attunements visualizes, draws or intones the names of any of the symbols, it can help them to connect with Reiki energy and activate the function and specific intention the symbol represents.

The distance attunements provided as a part of this course will activate within you an ability to work with different levels of Reiki through intention as well as by consciously invoking the symbols.

Although intention alone can activate the power connected with the symbols, you will want to ensure you study the meanings of each symbol. It is not necessary that you completely understand the meanings of the symbols before you begin using them but a basic understanding will deepen your experience when using them. The symbols can help to refine the focus of your Reiki sessions when used in your Reiki practice.

Over time, the attunement process has shifted since it was first taught. In the distant past, you would meet weekly with fellow members and a master, listen to a lecture and practice. You might also receive a Reiki session after which you would meditate. During your meditation, the Master would perform a Reiju which is an empowerment that helps you to deepen your connection to Reiki energy. If you were progressing, you may be invited to begin the second level of instruction.

The symbols hold more importance in Usui Shiki Ryoho Reiki from the Hayashi-Takata lineage. Information was passed along more quickly. Placing more emphasis on the symbols and hand positions helped students to connect with Reiki as they developed the ability to sense the energy in recipients. The Reiki Masters trained by Madam Takata trained were taught to keep the symbols private from non-practitioners. This practice has shifted as access to information has increased significantly.

The Traditional Usui Reiki Master Symbol

BALANCE THROUGH YOUR HIGHER SELF

大   DAI

光   KO

明   MYO

The Reiki Master Symbol

Pronounced dye-ko-me-o, the Dai Ko Myo (DKM) in Usui Reiki is known as the Master symbol. It is considered to be one of the most powerful symbols used in Reiki and can only be used by a Reiki Master. This symbol combines the power of Cho Ku Rei, Sei He Ki and Hon Sha Ze Sho Nen. The DKM symbol can access the highest vibration and can have a profound effect on the energetic aspects of the bodymind.

Using this symbol can help to address imbalances that the soul is carrying that are ready to be transmuted. By healing first at this energetic level, the mental and physical aspects of the bodymind are then balanced as well. The Dai Ko Myo symbol can also help to balance out energies that have been carried through inherited memory.

The Dai Ko Myo symbol represents the source of Reiki energy and can be translated as shining light, or enlightenment. This symbol is used in Buddhism and is found written in Buddhist temples; therefore, although it is sacred, it is not secret.

BALANCE THROUGH YOUR HIGHER SELF

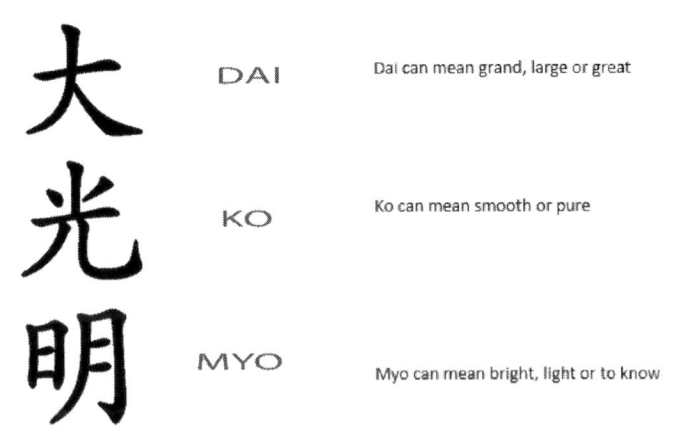

大 DAI — Dai can mean grand, large or great

光 KO — Ko can mean smooth or pure

明 MYO — Myo can mean bright, light or to know

There are variations of this symbol and you can explore them to see which one resonates with you most.

Remember that Reiki energy is very effective with or without the symbols. You can choose to use all four symbols in a session or none at all. Remember that these symbols are a tool to help you focus your energy.

You will want to be familiar with the symbols but do not want to rely on them. With time and practice, your energy will be focused with your intent and the symbols will not need to be an integral part of your session. Dr. Usui created Reiki with the intention that it be easy to learn and simple to administer. Usui created few rules and wanted to keep Reiki straightforward and uncomplicated. Reiki can be flexible to meet the needs of both the practitioner and the recipients, but Reiki does not need additional rules.

How to draw the DKM (Traditional)

BALANCE THROUGH YOUR HIGHER SELF

DAI

KO

MYO

Remember that it does not matter which version of the DKM you use, it is the intention that is important and all versions of the DKM symbol will work.

The Dai Ko Myo symbol represents empowering the connection to the soul. It enables recognition and clarity about your true path in life. The DKM master symbol is used in the attunement of others to Reiki.

Once you are attuned to the energy connected to DKM, you can use it for yourself and others each time you perform a Reiki session. The Master/Teacher attunement increases intuitive and psychic abilities and is said to work at a cellular level.

The DKM can also be a catalyst for creating dramatic changes in one's career and life. The DKM can also be used to help manifest your goals. You can do so by drawing, projecting or intoning the symbol and then visualizing what you intend to manifest into your life with the intention that you will receive what is in your highest good.

It is believed that disease originates first in the energy body. Reiki will help remove these blocks, restore energy and balance. This can contribute to healing on a physical, emotional, and mental level. You may find that you use the DKM frequently because it resonates at a high frequency and can have a positive effect in most situations. The DKM can also be used for protection and to clear away negativity.

Ways to Activate the Master Symbol

- Mentally beam a white DKM through your hands as you work with a client
- Visualize a white DKM on the palms of your hands before your session
- Draw the DKM with your tongue on the roof of your mouth and project it on the back of your hands as you perform your session
- Draw the DKM on your hands with your index finger before you begin your session
- Draw the DKM in the air and beam it in the direction of your hands

Where You Can Use the DKM in a Session

First you will want to draw or project the DKM symbol on your own hands (in the palms) and then draw or project the DKM on to the recipient. You may find using the DKM with the crown chakra to be powerful. Also if the recipient has any areas that are out of balance, the DKM can help to address the condition on a deep level. Using the DKM with the heart center and hands can also be an effective way to help the recipient strengthen their connection to their higher self.

Remember that intention is key so intoning the DKM silently (you can use the abbreviated version) is just as effective as any other method of activation.

Using the Dai Ko Myo

Dai Ko Myo can be translated as 'the great shining light'.

You have learned that the common definition of Reiki is 'universal life force'. You will also want to note that the kanji can also be translated to include 'universal life energy or spirit coming together through us'. In this translation it can represent our connection to everything around us.

During the master level, you learn the Dai Ko Myo symbol and begin to explore the concept that we are one with the universal life force. The true understanding of this does not come about through the attunement or a certificate, but through awareness. There is nothing you need to attain, there is no goal you must reach – just oneness with the perfection that you already are.

The DKM represents light and purity. This is source. Once you know the Dai Ko Myo symbol, you can use it for any intention and in place of all the other symbols. This will assist you in moving from relying on the symbols and using tools outside of yourself to being one with Reiki.

You can use the DKM in any situation you would want to use the other symbols. You can intone the name during meditation, while concentrating on all that is.

Variations of the DKM

There are a number of variations of the DKM symbol. You can choose the symbol that resonates most with you in your practice. As always, intention and understanding is the key.

Non Traditional Usui Reiki Master Symbols

There are a number of non-traditional Reiki Master symbols available that you can use if you choose. If you feel intuitively drawn to these symbols, try working with them and decide based on your experiences and your recipient's feedback.

Two Versions of the Dumo or the Tibetan Master Symbol

UNIFYING THE MIND AND
BODY WITH KUNDALINI FIRE

DUMO

RELEASING IMBALANCE
DUMO VERSION 2 / TIBETAN MASTER

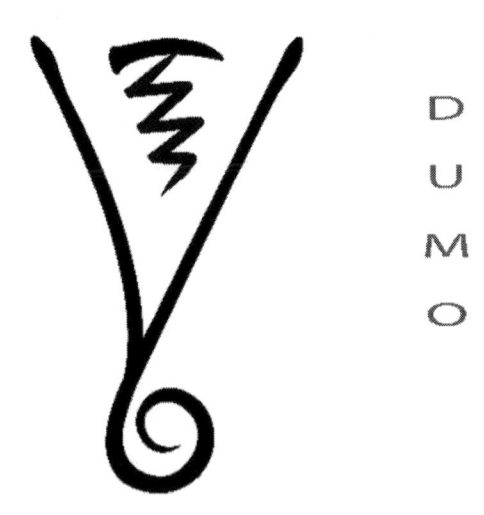

D
U
M
O

This symbol is pronounced 'doo moe" and represents the energy of the kundalini that rises up the spine as awareness increases. The Dumo symbol is thought to be the catalyst of the sacred flame or kundalini fire. It is said that Dumo works with the fire in the base/root chakra. You can use the Dumo symbol to release negative energy and imbalances from the body, a space, or situation. Practitioners that use crystals use the symbol to help clear them. The Dumo is also used in the attunement process in conjunction with the Violet Breath which you will explore.

Raku

GROUNDING OR IGNITING ENERGY ALONG THE SPINE

R
A
K
U

The Raku symbol or Tibetan Fire Serpent symbol is used before the attunement process and sessions in some branches of Reiki. This symbol can be used to ground when draw downwards and used to access the chakras when drawn in an upwards direction. In an attunement ceremony this symbol can be drawn along the back of the student.

The Reiki Attunement Ceremony

A Reiki attunement opens the energy pathways in the body which helps the student to channel Reiki energy more effectively. This heightened ability to channel Reiki is permanent and lasts for a lifetime.

It is important to note that the attunements alone do not make the student a Master. Time spent studying Reiki, performing self-treatments and adhering to the principles are needed. It is also key to remember that the practitioner is not the healer. The student is a vessel for Reiki energy which is the healer. The energy is drawn in by the recipient, directed by the wisdom of the bodymind that knows what needs to be addressed.

The attunement process and symbols used will vary from Reiki Master to Reiki Master. This is because for many years Masters were not allowed to take notes or keep copies of the symbols. Keep in mind that this does not affect the power or the effectiveness of the Reiki attunements. The recipient of the attunement should be relaxed, open and sets the intention to receive the initiation.

In order for a Reiki Master to successfully attune others to Reiki, the Master should be relaxed, with the intention that they will attune others successfully to Reiki so that they can go on to teach others.

You can ask your student to remove all jewellery, glasses and shoes if you choose. Some individuals argue that jewellery and metal can interfere with energy flow and that the metal holds energy. The removal of shoes is thought to assist in grounding during the attunement. In my experience, the ceremony can effectively be performed with jewellery and shoes.

During the ceremony, the student will sit on a chair with their feet flat on the floor. Their hands will be in front of their chest with their palms together in prayer position.

During the attunement ceremony, you are working with energy that has wisdom beyond understanding. As a Reiki master with experience you will allow yourself to be guided by your intuition more than procedure.

The Hui Yin and the Violet Breath

Although the Hui Yin and Violet Breath are generally not considered traditional Reiki techniques they are commonly used. You have the choice to use them when passing attunements as some feel that the attunements are more powerful when using these techniques.

The Hui Yin is a point associated with a qigong technique called the Microcosmic Orbit. When using this technique, it is thought that a higher frequency energy becomes a part of the attunement process. You can try using the techniques and see what responses you receive from your students. The attunements you receive in this course are performed using these techniques.

Please remember that your intention is key, so do not be concerned if you find it too difficult to use the Hui Yin and Violet Breath when performing your attunements. If you find that adding the Hui Yin and Violet Breath techniques complicate the attunement process do not use them. It is more important for you to be relaxed and present, with your focus on passing on the gift of Reiki. Dr. Usui did not use this process.

The Hui Yin

The Hui Yin point is an energetic location between the anus and the genitals and is the first point in the Ren meridian (Conception Vessel). It is the meeting place of three important meridians (Ren, Du and Chong-Conception, Governing and Penetrating). To perform the technique, the Hui Yin point is contracted, and the tongue is placed against the soft palate (behind the upper teeth).

In order to use the Hui Yin technique, you will want to practice developing the control needed to hold the point for periods of time. You can develop this control by contracting the muscles in this area. This is similar to pelvic floor exercises and Kegels. Be sure you begin these exercises slowly and contract gently. Please do not strain yourself. You can practice contracting these muscles continuously as you go through your day.

The Violet Breath

In order to perform the Violet Breath, you will visualize a white mist surrounding you. Then you will contract the Hui Yin and place your tongue behind your upper teeth. Breathe in and imagine a white light coming through your crown chakra, down the front of the body, through the Hui Yin and up along the spine to the centre of your head.

Now imagine the white mist filling your head and visualize the white mist turning blue, and then indigo and watch the energy begin to swirl in a clockwise direction. As the mist swirls, watch it turn to violet.

Within the violet mist visualize the golden Dumo symbol. Next, blow the Dumo symbol and Violet Breath into the student's chakras including the crown chakra where you will project the symbol as you silently intone the name of the symbol.

Non-Traditional Reiki Attunements

There is an attunement process known as the crown to crown attunement and I first came across it when studying with Masters Adele and Garry Malone. This attunement is a simple way to attune another person to Reiki energy. You will activate all the Reiki symbols by projecting them above your student's head and then stating or setting the intention that you will attune this individual to a specific level of Reiki. You will then allow the power and wisdom of Reiki to work with the energetic body of the student and observe the attunement ceremony.

An example of the intention is "Reiki, the universal life force energy will now attune _____ (recipients' name) to Reiki level one in the interests of their highest good".

Once you have set the intention, the energy will flow into your crown chakra and through your body and then flow through the student's aura and in through their crown chakra. The crown to crown attunement can clear blockages, so that the students is a clearer channel for Reiki energy. You will always want to set the intention that the crown to crown attunement be for the highest good of the recipient and all concerned. The length of this attunement can vary so you will close the ceremony when you intuitively feel called to.

As you observe the energy flowing through you and to your student, you can observe as the energy flows through each of their chakras as they open and clear. You will witness this ceremony with the understanding that the student will now have access to Reiki energy for their lifetime whenever they feel called to use it for themselves and others.

There are no different actions in a crown to crown attunement for Level I, versus Level II and Master. The only difference is in your intention. For the first degree your focus will be on allowing the Reiki energy to flow through the student and for their body to release any energy/beliefs or memories that are not serving them.

In Level II, you will intend that the student will have an energetic understanding of the Level II symbols and will be able to work with them effectively when they choose to.

With the Master Level, your focus will be on observing the student connect with the Master Symbol so that they can work with it as well as have the ability to attune others to Reiki energy.

Over time in this ceremony as well as the traditional ceremony, you may start to sense the energetic shifts as they occur in the students you work with. These sensations can vary and can include but are not limited to colors, temperature, images etc. You can just observe the information and know that even if you do not receive any messages or sensations that Reiki energy is successfully completing the ceremony.

Just as every single Reiki session is different, each attunement ceremony will have its own nuances. In every case, they are perfect and what the bodymind of the recipient in connection with Reiki energy is choosing to experience.

This type of attunement ceremony can take anywhere from ten to twenty minutes (or longer) depending on if you perform any additional balancing work with the Reiki energy and recipient.

The energy will diminish as the session comes to a close. If you do not feel a change in the energy, you can intuitively choose when to finish. You may find performing attunements in your mental Reiki room very helpful as you can access more information there. In your mental Reiki room, you can ask if the attunement ceremony is complete.

Once you know the ceremony is closing you will set the intention that the energetic connection between you and the student is now severed and with gratitude set the intention that they will move forward as confident and powerful Reiki Practitioners/Masters.

Preparing for the Reiki Attunement Ceremony

The key to a successful attunement ceremony is that the recipient is open to receiving Reiki energy. Your intention as the Reiki master to pass on the gift of Reiki also needs to be clear.

The ceremony you will explore now is also simple and straightforward. It is recommended that you explore the various ways of attuning students and see which one feels right for you at this time. Occasionally you can revisit the other methods and see if you would like to adopt a new way of attuning students.

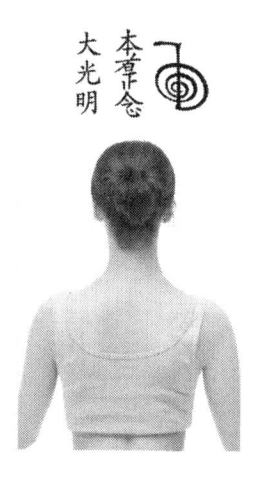

Remember that each of these versions will be effective. It is important that you choose the one that feels best for you and your students.

Master Preparation

Keep in mind that during the ceremony you will be in close contact with your students for a prolonged period of time. It is important that you and your clothes are clean, that your teeth are brushed/mouth fresh and that you do not have any strong colognes or perfumes on. This will ensure that your student is focused on the energy rather than your proximity to them.

The room you will be performing the attunements in needs to be clean and fresh. Ideally you have some time to open the windows before the ceremony if possible to bring fresh air in. The room is ideally free of clutter and feels inviting. You can use the Reiki symbols if you feel called to in order to balance the energy in the room before the ceremony.

Students will ideally be sitting in chairs during the ceremony. If you have a group of students, you can arrange the chairs in a circle with enough room in between each chair so that you have the ability to move around each student. The chairs can be facing outward so the students can have their privacy as they receive their attunements. If the room is smaller, having the chairs in a line is also an option. If you would prefer to perform each attunement privately, you can have a separate room where students meditate and wait for their ceremony. When a student is finished, they can return to the room and reflect quietly on the ceremony.

When the student is ready to receive their attunements you will ensure that their feet are flat on the floor. Their hands will be in prayer position in front of their heart chakra. You will ask the student to close their eyes and take a few deep breaths. You can let them know that you will be moving around their chair as you perform the ceremony. You can also let the student know that you will be touching the student's shoulders, moving their hands at some point and blowing/tapping the symbols into the palms of their hands. You can clarify that you will only be touching the students shoulders and hands.

Then you are both ready to begin the ceremony. You will complete it using the method you choose as outlined in upcoming sections.

Once the ceremony is complete, you can provide students with the option to share their experience with their classmates if they choose. This can be done as a large group or in smaller groups if the students are more reserved. In some cases, a change of scenery such as moving outside or into a break room can be helpful.

How to Perform Reiki Attunements

In this lesson we will look at how to attune your Reiki students. You will want to prepare for the attunement and have your student sitting in a chair with their eyes closed and their hands in the prayer position ready for the attunement.

Step 1: Prepare yourself and your student

- You will stand in front of your student approximately 2-3 feet away from them.

- Ask your student to close their eyes and raise their hands in the prayer position with hands in front of their heart chakra.

- Silently set a short intention (example: "I call upon Reiki, the universal life force, all the Reiki masters past, present and future (remember Reiki is not bound by time or space) especially Dr Usui, Dr Hayashi and Madam Takata to participate in this attunement ceremony for (insert students name). I ask that the power and wisdom of Reiki guides and assists me to pass on the gift of Reiki through this attunement of (insert students' name) to Usui Reiki Level (I, II or Master depending on the attunements). I ask that this ceremony is an uplifting and inspiring experience for (insert students' name) so that (insert students' name) can move forward as a confident and powerful Reiki practitioner.

- When you feel ready and can sense the Reiki energy around you, open your eyes.

- Draw (1x) and intone (3x) the DKM and CKR on **your palms**

- Draw (1x) and intone (3x) the CKR in **front of your body**, intending that your chakras open to receive Reiki.

- Draw (1x) and intone (3x) the DKM, CKR, SHK and HSZSN **above the student** intending for the energy to fill the room. **These symbols will be called on as needed during the ceremony**.

- Ask your student to take a deep relaxing breath as they perform a silent invocation opening themselves up to receiving the Reiki attunement (example: I (students name) call upon Reiki, the universal life force. I am ready and open to receive the Reiki attunement). Give your student a few moments to complete the silent invocation. When you sense they are ready you can continue.

- Ask your student to relax, follow your directions and enjoy the experience of the Reiki attunement ceremony.

Step 2: Opening your student up to receive Reiki

- Now walk around counter clockwise to the back of your student.

- Raise your hands in the prayer position in front of your heart chakra.

- Move closer to your student and place your NON-dominant hand on your student's shoulder.

- If you choose to include the Hui Yin and Violet Breath in your attunement you will do as follows. Place your tongue behind your top front teeth at the roof of your mouth and contract the Hui Yin to boost the flow of Reiki in and around your body. (**PLEASE NOTE**: This technique is optional, you do not need to do this and it will not affect the success of the attunements. It is done in this course because this is the way your Master was taught during training. Many Reiki masters do not use this technique during the attunement ceremony. Try it and if you like it using this technique you can continue to use it. If not, do not include it as a part of your attunement ceremony. Remember that intention is key.)

Step 3: Opening student up to receive Reiki (Crown chakra)

- **Standing behind the Reiki student**
- Now you will raise your dominant hand and hold it horizontally above your Reiki student's **crown chakra**.
- Draw a small CKR above the student's crown chakra to open the student's crown centre.
- Now place your cupped hands over the student's crown chakra and beam/channel the three previously drawn Reiki symbols (DKM + HSZSN + CKR) into the students crown chakra filling their whole head with Reiki energy. *Remember to silently intone the names of each of the symbols three times.*

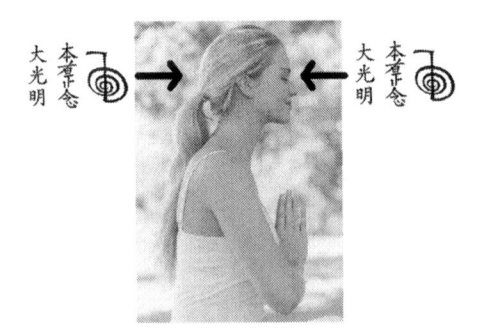

Step 4: Opening student up to receive Reiki (Third eye chakra)

- **Standing at the right hand side of the Reiki student)**
- Draw a small CKR over the student's **third eye chakra** to open the student's third eye centre.
- Now with your right hand a few inches in front of the student's third eye chakra and your left hand a few inches behind the student's head beam the three previously drawn Reiki symbols (DKM + HSZSN + CKR) into the student's third eye chakra filling their third eye centre with Reiki energy. *Remember to silently intone the names of each of the symbols three times.*

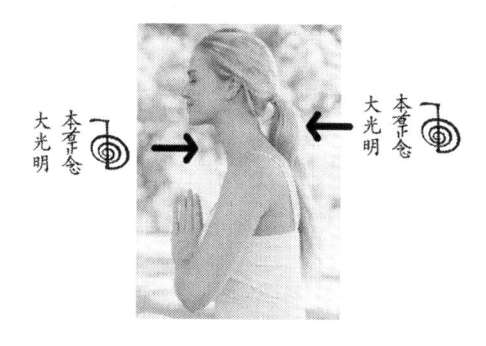

Step 5: Opening student up to receive Reiki (Throat chakra)

- **Standing at the right hand side of the Reiki student**
- Draw a small CKR over the student's throat chakra to open the student's throat centre.
- With your right hand a few inches in front of the student's throat chakra and your left hand a few inches behind the back of the student's neck beam the three previously drawn Reiki symbols (DKM + HSZSN + CKR) into the students throat chakra filling their throat centre with Reiki energy. *Remember to silently intone the names of each of the symbols three times.*

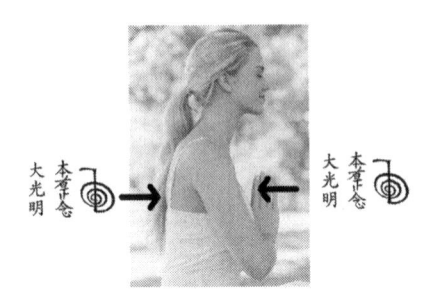

Step 6: Opening student up to receive Reiki (Heart chakra)

- **Move so you are standing in front of the Reiki student**
- Draw a small CKR over the students Heart Chakra to open the student's Heart centre.
- Now with your cupped hands side by side thumbs together facing toward your student's heart chakra; beam the three previously drawn Reiki symbols (DKM + HSZSN + CKR) into the student's heart chakra, filling their heart centre with Reiki energy. *Remember to silently intone the names of each of the symbols three times.*

Step 7: Opening student up to receive Reiki (Solar plexus, sacral and root chakras as well as body)

- **Standing in front of the Reiki student**
- Leaving the student's hands in the prayer position, step back slightly and draw a small CKR over the student's solar plexus, sacral and root chakras to open the student's remaining three energy centres.
- Now with your cupped hands side by side with thumbs together facing towards your student's solar plexus, sacral and root chakras, beam the three previously drawn Reiki symbols (DKM + HSZSN + CKR) into the student's solar plexus, sacral and root chakras filling their three energy centres with Reiki energy. *Remember to silently intone the names of each of the symbols three times.*

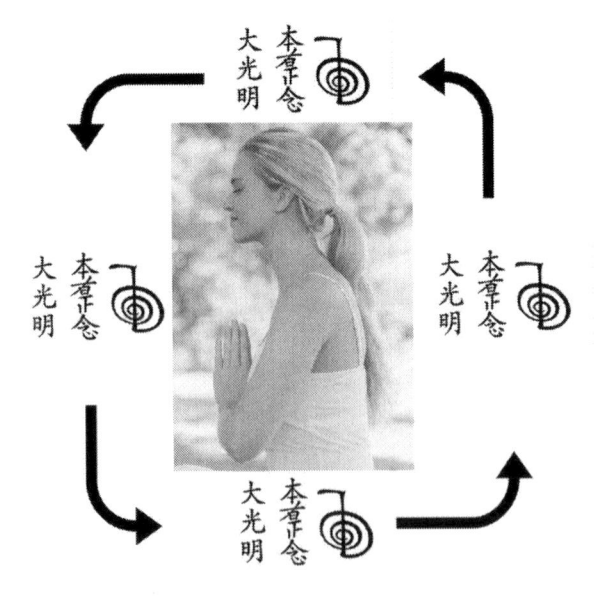

- Next beam/channel the three previously drawn Reiki symbols (DKM + HSZSN + CKR) into the students' arms, chest, abdomen, thighs, legs and feet. Visualize Reiki energy filling every muscle, organ, tissue and cell of their body. *Remember to silently intone the names of each of the symbols three times.*

Level I - Cho Ku Rei

Level II - Cho Ku Rei, Sei He Ki, Hon Sha Ze Sho Nen

Master Level - Cho Ku Rei, Sei He Ki, Hon Sha Ze Sho Nen, Dai Ko Myo

Step 8: Attuning the student to the symbols

- Open the student's hands like a book and draw the symbols into the palms of their hands and then tapping three times.
    - Level I: Draw CKR in both palms and tap three times
    - Level II: Draw CKR, SHK, and HSZSN in both palms and tap three times
    - Level III: Draw CKR, SHK, HSZSN and DKM and tap three times
- Fold the student's hands back into prayer position.

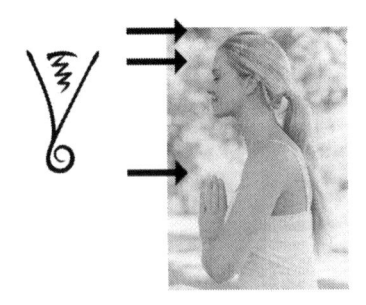

Step 9: Violet Breath

- **Standing in front of the Reiki student**
- Now place your hands around the student's hands and move them so that their fingertips are in line with their heart chakra.
- Blow the Violet Breath from the **root chakra to the crown chakra**.

Step 10: Closing the ceremony

- **Standing in front of the Reiki student**
- Take the student's hands and move them down so that they are resting on their lap.
- Draw a large CKR over the front of your Reiki student's body to ground their energy.

- Place your hands a few inches above their crown chakra within their auric field. Starting from the crown chakra, run your hands down both sides of their aura until you reach their feet. Touch the floor with both hands to complete the grounding and break the connection with the Reiki student.

- Finally, silently set an intention of gratitude to Reiki. (Example: Thanks be given to Reiki, the universal life force, Dr Usui, Dr Hayashi and Madam Takata as well as all Reiki masters past, present and future for taking part in this attunement ceremony for "insert students name". I ask that the power and wisdom of Reiki nurture and guide "insert students name" from this point forward empowering "insert students name" to be a powerful and confident Reiki Practitioner.

- Allow as much time to pass as you intuitively feel necessary, then say to the student: "You can now come back to full awareness in your own time whenever you are ready" or "This concludes the first degree attunement."

- You can take some time and ask the student to talk about the feelings, visions or experiences that he/she had during the attunement. This discussion allows the student to process what has occurred and helps if he/she needs to validate that "the attunement worked".

If several people are being attuned this sharing can be done after all have been completed. You may find it helpful to instruct the student if they are part of a group being attuned to continue to keep their hands resting on their lap and close their eyes once more and go inside and relax while waiting for the attunement to be completed on their fellow students.

Performing Each Attunement Separately

If you prefer to perform each attunement separately, below are the steps you can complete. The purpose of an attunement or Reiju is to align the student's energy level to resonate with their higher self which will make them a clear channel for Reiki energy.

Level I First Attunement

This attunement opens the crown chakra to access and channel more Reiki energy which will assist in aligning the student's physical body to resonate at their natural frequency.

Step 1

Standing behind student

Raise your non dominant hand with your palm open. With your dominant hand draw the Dai Ko Myo (Master Symbol) over the student's crown chakra

Step 2

Place your dominant hand above the student's crown chakra while your non dominant hand remains extended. Visualize the Cho Ku Rei, Sei Hei Ki, and Hon Sha Ze Sho Nen symbols. Hold that position for a moment, allowing the energy to flow.

Step 3

Walk counter-clockwise to the front of the student. Using your non dominant hand, raise the student's hands up to a position easier for you to work with. While still clasping the student's hands, bend down to eye level with the student's hands and place your dominant hand fingertips to the student's fingertips. Maintain that position while visualizing the CKR, SHK, HSZSN and DKM.

Step 4

In the same hand position, lift the student's hands up to their face so you can access their throat chakra. Visualize the CKR and breathe in through your nose. Moving from the heart chakra, throat chakra and third eye chakra blow out over the three chakras.

Step 5

Place the student's hands over their heart center and take a step back. Take some time to be present and when you feel ready you can conclude the attunement. You may wish to let the student know the attunement is completed by saying something such as, "this concludes the first attunement." You can take some time and ask the student to talk about the feelings, visions or experiences that he/she had during the attunement. This discussion allows the student to process what has occurred and helps if he/she needs to validate that "the attunement worked".

Level I Second & Third Attunements

This attunement opens the student's throat and third eye chakras with the intent of balancing the functioning of the nervous system to enhance clear thinking and the ability to communicate personal truth.

The steps you will complete for the second and third attunements are the same. You will begin by walking counter clockwise to back of the student.

Step 1

Raise your non dominant hand with palm open and facing upwards. With your dominant hand draw the DKM over the student's crown chakra.

Step 2

Place both hands on the student's shoulders and visualize the CKR, SHK and HSZSN. Observe the energy flowing through the student's chakras from crown to root.

Step 3

Walk counter-clockwise to the front of the student. Using your non dominant hand, pull the student's hands up and bend to the student's eye level. Place your dominant hand's fingertips to the student's fingertips. Visualize the CKR, SHK, HSZSN and DKM.

Step 4

In the same hand position, lift the student's hands up to their face so you can access their throat chakra. Visualize the CKR and breathe in through your nose. Moving from the heart chakra, throat chakra and third eye chakra blow out over the three chakras.

Step 5

Place the student's hands over their heart center and take a step back. Take some time to be present and when you feel ready you can conclude the attunement. You may wish to let the student know the attunement is completed by saying something such as, "this concludes the first attunement." You can take some time and ask the student to talk about the feelings, visions or experiences that he/she had during the attunement. This discussion allows the student to process what has occurred and helps if he/she needs to validate that "the attunement worked"

Level I Fourth Attunement

You will use the same preparation methods as with the first, second and third attunements. The student is sitting in a chair with hands in front of their heart in Gassho position. This attunement addresses the student's third eye and crown chakra, with a focus on higher consciousness and intuition.

Step 1

Raise your non dominant arm with your palm facing upwards and open. With your dominant hand draw the DKM above the student's crown chakra.

Step 2

Move counter clockwise to the side of the student's chair. Place one hand in front of the student's forehead and the other hand behind the back of the student's head. Visualize the CKR, SHK, HSZSN and DKM.

Step 3

Walk counter-clockwise to the front of the student. Using your non dominant hand, pull the student's hands up and bend to the student's eye level. Place your dominant hand's fingertips to the student's fingertips. Visualize the CKR, SHK, HSZSN and DKM.

Step 4

In the same hand position, lift the student's hands up to their face so you can access their throat chakra. Visualize the CKR and breathe in through your nose. Moving from the heart chakra, throat chakra and third eye chakra blow out over the three chakras.

Step 5

Place the student's hands over their heart center and take a step back. Take some time to be present and when you feel ready you can conclude the attunement. You may wish to let the student know the attunement is completed by saying something such as, "this concludes the first attunement." You can take some time and ask the student to talk about the feelings, visions or experiences that he/she had during the attunement. This discussion allows the student to process what has occurred and helps if he/she needs to validate that "the attunement worked"

Level II Attunement

The Level II attunement seals the symbols into the student's hands.

Step 1

Raise your non dominant arm with your palm facing upwards and open. With your dominant hand draw the DKM above the student's crown chakra.

Step 2

Move counter clockwise to the side of the student's chair. Place one hand in front of the student's forehead and the other hand behind the back of the student's head. Visualize the CKR, SHK, and HSZSN.

Step 3

Walk counter-clockwise to the front of the student. Using your non dominant hand, pull the student's hands up and bend to the student's eye level. Place your dominant hand's fingertips to the student's fingertips. Visualize the DKM.

Step 4

Open the student's hands and place them on their lap with palms facing upwards. Take one hand and draw the HSZSN with your dominant hand over their palm and place their hand within both of yours. Draw the SHK over the student's palm and place their hand within both of yours. Now draw the CKR over the student's palm and place their hand within both of yours. Return the student's hand to their lap. Raise the student's other hand and repeat all of this step four on the second hand.

Step 5

In the same hand position, lift the student's hands up to their face so you can access their throat chakra. Visualize the CKR and breathe in through your nose. Moving from the heart chakra, throat chakra and third eye chakra blow out over the three chakras.

Step 6

Place the student's hands over their heart center and take a step back. Take some time to be present and when you feel ready you can conclude the attunement. You may wish to let the student know the attunement is completed by saying something such as, "this concludes the first attunement." You can take some time and ask the student to talk about the feelings, visions or experiences that he/she had during the attunement. This discussion allows the student to process what has occurred and helps if he/she needs to validate that "the attunement worked"

Master Level Attunement

In the Master/Teacher Level, the student is attuned to the Master symbol Dai Ko Myo, through one attunement. The focus of this attunement is to enable the student to manifest insightful vision and compassion with the intent of helping others.

Before this attunement, the Master and student will spend time in meditation to connect to the Reiki energy. Once the connection has been made, the ceremony will begin. The student will be sitting in a chair with hands in Gassho position.

Step 1

Walk counter clockwise to the back of the student. Take a deep breath and hold it, while placing the tip of your tongue behind your upper front teeth. Raise your non dominant arm with your palm facing upwards and open. With your dominant hand, draw the DKM over the student's crown chakra. Reach forward with both hands and clasp the student's hands and release your breath, blowing above the student's head into the student's crown chakra.

Step 2

Perform all four of the Level I attunements using the DKM symbol. You will blow into the student's crown chakra before moving to the front of the student to work with their hands. This means that the held breath will be blown into the Crown Chakra four more times from the back of the student.

Step 3

Perform the Level II attunement using the DKM. Blow into the student's crown chakra before walking to side of student. Once you have drawn the three symbols and placed the student's hands within your own, draw the DKM into the student's hands and place within yours. You will then blow from the student's root chakra up through the other chakras to the third-eye chakra.

Step 4

Place the student's hands over their heart center and take a step back. Take some time to be present and when you feel ready you can conclude the attunement. You may wish to let the student know the attunement is completed by saying something such as, "this concludes the first attunement." You can take some time and ask the student to talk about the feelings, visions or experiences that he/she had during the attunement. This discussion allows the student to process what has occurred and helps if he/she needs to validate that "the attunement worked"

Distance Reiki Attunements

Although some Reiki masters find distance attunements controversial, thousands of Reiki students who have received distance attunements have demonstrated that they are just as effective as attunements received in person. Keep in mind that the distance attunements operate under the same principles as a Reiki distance session as taught in Level II, so masters who are against distance attunements are also questioning the principles that they themselves are teaching in Reiki Level II.

In this day and age where information is accessible from any part of the world and our understanding of the flexible nature of time and space, it makes sense that distance attunements are becoming commonplace.

If you choose, you can set up distance attunements with your students, you can do so through email, phone or a form on your website.

In cases where an individual is ill without access to a practitioner nearby and would like to receive Reiki, they can be attuned from a distance so they can perform Reiki on themselves. Although it would be more ideal for them to take the course so they have an awareness of the energy they are working with, in cases where that is not possible working with the Reiki energy can still be very effective.

You can choose to attune all of your students to all three levels of Reiki at once using the combined Reiki I, II and III distance attunement techniques. Or you can choose to offer individual distance attunements.

Benefits of Performing Reiki Distance Attunements

It is important to remember that in addition to the attunements (whether from a distance or in-person) the student needs to commit to deepening their understanding of Reiki, performing their daily self-treatments and continue to practice Reiki both in their lives and when working with others.

The attunements are like being given a key to a doorway that leads to unimaginable treasures. It is up to the student to take the initiative and walk through the door. The key will always be with them but they will need to take action through self-treatments, introspection and working with others to explore the gift that is Reiki.

You may want to set some goals for yourself as you near the end of this course. These could include performing daily self-treatments, meditating on the 5 principles, performing a certain number of sessions with others and exploring additional reading and courses.

Preparing to Perform Distance Attunements

When you perform distance attunements, you are more keenly aware of how connected we all are. As always, the intention of the Master and student are what ensures the success of the ceremony.

If you choose to offer distance attunements, you will want to practice and explore the various methods to see what feels right for you.

Mental Reiki Room

This method involves you entering your mental Reiki room and then inviting the student in. You will perform the ceremony just as you would in-person with the exception that you are doing so in your mental Reiki room through your mind's eye.

This method is very effective and you will likely find that you can access more information in this mental space. This method also allows you to focus on Reiki energy rather than the physical level.

Surrogate

With this method, you would perform the ceremony using either a person or object as the surrogate. This could be a friend or family member, teddy bear, ball etc. First you will set the intention that the surrogate is a representative for your student. Then you will perform the ceremony as you would in person on the surrogate. Please refer back to the Reiki Level 2 Manual for more information on how to use a surrogate.

Using Information to Connect During a Distance Attunement

If when performing attunements, you would prefer to project yourself to your student's location, you can use information and technology to help you do so. For example, if you student lives in Sedona Arizona you can use the maps on your internet browser to help you see their location.

With that location in mind, you can allow Reiki to connect you across time and space to perform the ceremony at your student's location in your mind's eye.

Steps to Performing the Distance Attunement

1. First you will choose which distance attunement method you will use.
2. Then you will choose a date and time that works best for you and your student.
3. The student will be in a comfortable space and they are open to receive the attunements at the agreed upon time.
4. You will ground and center yourself as you normally would before a session or ceremony.
5. You will connect with the recipient using the method you choose. Regardless of method you will visualize the student and the Reiki energy that is being drawn through you by them so that they can receive the attunements.
6. Once you feel energetically connected to the student you will perform the ceremony.
7. If the student has any questions or concerns, they know they can connect with you.

How the Recipient Should Prepare for the Attunement

Here are some ways your students can prepare for their distance attunement ceremony.

The student can choose a time where they will be able to relax for around 30 minutes. Inevitably, there will be times when a student is distracted or interrupted during a ceremony. This is acceptable and is usually a way that the student's conscious mind is distracted so the energetic body can complete the work. If a student does contact you because they for whatever reason were not present during their ceremony, you can assure them that it occurred exactly as they needed it to. Animals and children may sometimes want to be in the same room during the ceremony as they sense the positive energy.

The student should choose a place that feels positive for them. This can be outdoors or in a place they feel peaceful and at ease. They can choose to play music if they wish. Ideally the student is comfortable in loose clothing and if they choose can remove their jewellery.

The student should avoid recreational mind-altering substances for 24 hours prior to the ceremony. Those substances such as coffee, alcohol and drugs (recreational) do not impact the energy but will affect the student's perception. Students can continue their doctor prescribed medications.

The student needs to be open to receiving the attunements. Intention is important. The only time in my humble experience that there has been an issue when performing a distance attunement is when the student did not truly wish to receive the energy. This in most cases is remedied by the student taking some time to reflect on why that might be and then rescheduling when they are truly ready.

The student does not need technology to receive the attunements. Although some Masters will perform the ceremony over video calls or the telephone, I have found that it takes away focus from the energy. You can use technology if you wish but know that it does not enhance the effectiveness of the attunements.

The student can close their eyes and focus on their breath during the ceremony. At the beginning they can set their intention such as: "I am open to receiving Reiki energy through these attunements so that I can balance and heal on all levels".

Once the ceremony is complete, the student can take time to resume their day. They need to ensure they are hydrated as their body processes the energy and they will want to begin their daily self-treatments.

Student Experiences during the Attunement Ceremony

The most common question you will receive as a Reiki Master after an attunement ceremony is: "this happened during the ceremony, or I felt this way during the ceremony…is that normal?" Just as everyone experiences Reiki sessions differently and the sensations will change for the same person from session to session, the attunement ceremony will provide a different experience for each student in each situation. The key point that you want to convey is that there is no right way to experience Reiki and the shifts associated with it and the body in connection with the energy will provide the experience that the student needs to have.

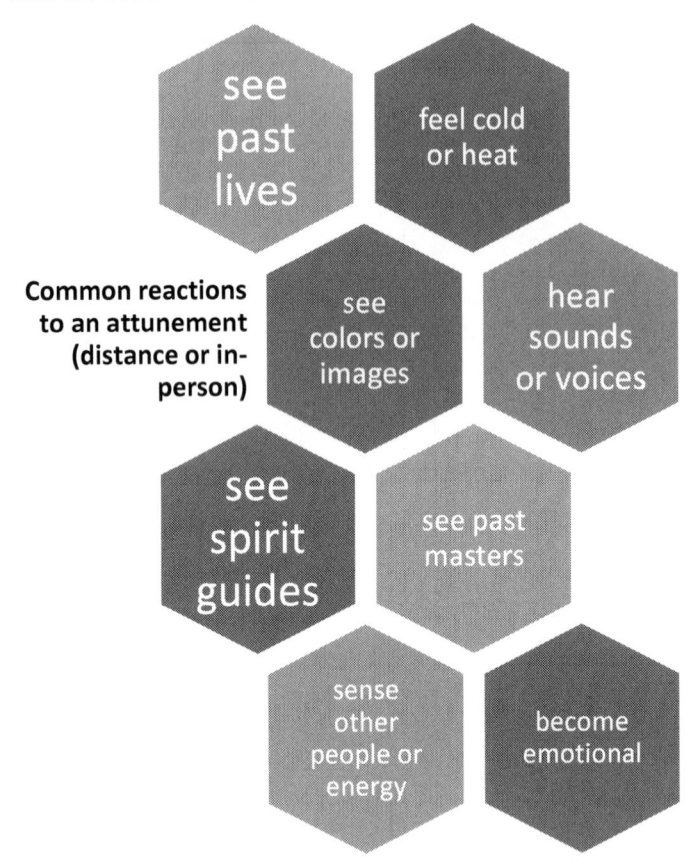

Common reactions to an attunement (distance or in-person)
- see past lives
- feel cold or heat
- see colors or images
- hear sounds or voices
- see spirit guides
- see past masters
- sense other people or energy
- become emotional

I have seen countless students enter the ceremony with expectations around what they want the ceremony to feel and look like, only to be discontent with how the ceremony actually ended up proceeding. Expectations in Reiki sessions, attunements and even life cloud our perception and prevent us from appreciating what is actually occurring for us in the present moment. I have also had students go into the ceremony with no expectations and even with the intention that they plan to sleep during the ceremony, only to find that the ceremony is full of information and sensations for them. In all cases the ceremony was effective. Remember that the body will create the experience that will benefit the student most. You and your students need to trust Reiki and the wisdom of their bodymind.

Advanced Reiki Techniques

Psychic Surgery

In our natural state, we have the ability to heal ourselves. Our bodies regenerate at a rapid rate and we can use this ability to ensure that the regeneration is in accordance with our healthy and balanced way of being. What prevents us from healing and regenerating a healthy body is the energy, beliefs and memories that we store in our tissues at a cellular level. By releasing this energy from the body, the body is then free to perform as it was intended to.

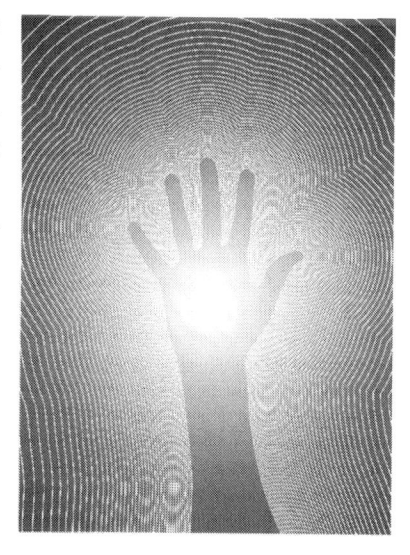

Although psychic surgery has been reserved for the esoteric, it is a simple technique you can use with yourself and others to remove the imbalances at the root energetic level so that the physical and emotional body can repair and heal. You can use this technique for any imbalance in the body and life. Usually one will be a reflection of the other.

Although the term surgery is used here, it is important to note that in addition to this technique the individual should be sure they are seeking additional support in the form of traditional allopathic care and professional counselling. This technique can assist on the energetic level but we need to ensure that the person is receiving additional support as they process and heal.

You may wish to perform this technique as a part of your Reiki sessions.

Visualization

The first part of this technique involves the client and has them locate and describe the issue. Whether the issue is a bad relationship, a problem with their work or a physical or emotional imbalance, the client will find where in the body this condition resonates and provide a description of it.

Once the client is clear on what the issue they would like to focus on is, you can ask them some guiding questions. You do not have to have the client tell you what the issue is, they only need to have it clear in their mind. The goal of the questions is to get the client familiar with the energy they are working with so they can assist in the release of it.

You will ask the client to mentally scan their body as they think of the issue and see where in their body they can feel it most. This can be tension that they sense or heat or cold. If the client is having difficulties locating the area, reassure them that is fine and to keep scanning until they feel an area resonate. If more than one area resonates you will complete the steps below for each area.

Once the client has focused on an area in their body you will ask them to describe the energy associated with the imbalance. This can include texture, color, size, smell, shape etc. Your questions can be in the form of: "If the energy of this imbalance had a (message, color, size etc.) what would it be?" It is acceptable if the client cannot answer all of the questions. You can move on to the next if they are struggling.

Now that the client has a tangible thing he/she can focus on, you will confirm with the client that they are ready to release this energy so that they can heal on all levels. This step is important because sometimes we unconsciously identify with our imbalances and on some level are not ready not release them. If the client is ready, you can reassure them that the wisdom they were supposed to take from this will be integrated as they move forward.

The Technique

You can choose to have your client lying down or seated in a chair. You will begin by drawing the CKR on the palms of your hands, silently intoning the name three times and tapping each palm of your hand with the index and middle finger of your other hand. You will draw a large CKR symbol along the front of the client's body while intoning the name CKR three times. Then you will draw a CKR symbol over each of your client's chakras as you intone the name CKR.

Allow Reiki to flow through you until you are beaming it from your entire body. Now focus on your hands. You will feel the Reiki energy extending out through your fingers making them longer. Move your hands slowly as you get used to your Reiki fingers. Your fingers can extend one to two hand lengths and will adjust as you need them to during the technique. You will draw or visualize the CKR on each of your Reiki fingers while intoning the name CKR.

Before you begin you will focus and remember that the recipient's body uses the Reiki energy with its own inner wisdom so that what is balanced is done so for the highest good of the recipient.

With the client focused on the area they feel is connected to the imbalance you will draw a CKR there as well while intoning the name CKR three times.

With your Reiki fingers, you will energetically reach inside the body and scoop out the dissonant energy. You may find your intuition guides you regarding the direction you use to gather the energy as well as how you remove it. As you are gathering the energy, make sure you are breathing normally. With the energy out of the recipient's body you will observe that energy as it shifts and becomes light energy that the universe will use in new ways.

You may find that you need to energetically go in and gather the dissonant energy more than once. When you feel intuitively that it has been cleared you can ask the client if they feel anything has shifted. You can ask them how the size, color, shape etc. has changed. If you are finding there is resistance, you may need to have the client reflect on what the message is behind the imbalance. You can help them by visualizing and intoning the SHK symbol above the area. Allow Reiki energy to flow through the symbol and wait with the client as they explore what the message is. Usually within a short amount of time there is a realization and emotions may arise. You will want to have tissues handy as the client may release those stored emotions through tears.

Now you will fill the area that housed the dissonant energy with Reiki energy. See the area filling up with light Reiki energy and set the intention that the bodymind is free of the imbalance.

You will confirm with the client that they feel the imbalance has shifted and you will energetically close the connection between you and the client.

You will watch as your Reiki fingers shorten and give thanks to Reiki energy. If you feel called to, you can perform a Reiki session after you have performed the technique.

This technique is very powerful because it accompanies the inherent understanding that everything that happens to us, happens for us. When we resist something, we take a piece of it and store it. Over time that storage begins to rule our way of being until the suffering is great enough that we seek an alternative way of being as a way of finding relief. This technique can help us to find that new way of being while taking the wisdom from the events we initially resisted.

Accessing Different Levels of Consciousness

By now, you have spent time practicing Reiki on yourself and likely others. You have heard positive feedback from your recipients and are gaining confidence. One of the wonderful things about Reiki is that although it is simple, it is profound.

This lesson will show you how you can use an existing tool, the CKR symbol in an advanced technique to help work with clients on a deeper level.

As your understanding of life and energy deepens, so will your practice. You will notice that many Reiki Masters create new systems of Reiki as their own awareness expands. In reality, the Reiki energy was always there and the power and wisdom of Reiki did not change, it is the understanding of the Practitioner that shifted. This is to remind you to go within when you are feeling called to take your awareness to the next level. Rather than trying to find a new method or system to quench your craving, come back to the fundamental lessons in Reiki and look inside yourself. Every single imbalance that we have can be effectively addressed through introspection.

We are beginning to understand that our perception creates our reality. For more resources regarding this notion, please visit the external resources section of this lecture.

Practitioners inevitably ask, "If I am the projector of my reality, why is my world not the way I wish it to be?" One reason is because more personal work is needed to clear away the sub-conscious programming. This can be done through Reiki sessions and meditating on the 5 principles. Another reason is because we are operating within a set of parameters we have agreed to in our society and as a species. Although there are many individuals who operate outside of these boundaries, for example people who no longer need to eat or individuals who can break the laws of physics at will, the majority of us for the time being are playing in the ball park. This consensus allows us all to play together so that we can grow and learn while enjoying the game of life.

In your practice however, you may find the need to break out of that set of agreed upon rules from time to time to help the recipient engage in healing that they would not otherwise be able to do under the standard operating procedures in this reality.

As you recall in Level II, the CKR symbol is seen as an amplifier. It is used to increase power during a Reiki session as well as activate the other symbols. In the Non-Traditional Symbols section in your manual, the reverse CKR is illustrated. You will notice that the spiral of the reverse CKR is clockwise. Where the traditional CKR is thought to dis-create and release dissonant energy, the clockwise CKR is thought to bring in resonant energy.

If you view the 3D version of the CKR spiral, it can be seen as shown. Spirals are seen throughout nature within and outside ourselves.

Spin can create a torsion field. These fields are thought to transmit energy and information. As applied here, these torsion fields have the capacity to create a paradigm shift which could lead to greater consciousness and awareness. As physics proves that multitudes of possibilities exist in potential, we are understanding that our perception collapses those possibilities into a single outcome. Using the power symbol in 3D with this understanding give the recipient's bodymind the option to access different levels of their awareness which will then help them to create a different reality. There is much research being done regarding spirals, vortexes and torsion fields. Feel free to explore.

The technique is as follows:

Once you are centered and have the recipient relaxed, you can ask them to focus on their breath and you ensure you are breathing smoothly and deeply while remaining comfortable.

You will perform a complete Reiki session. Whenever you feel called to, you will visualize a 3D CKR over the recipient's body in the place that feels appropriate. Trust that Reiki energy will guide the CKR to the place it needs to be. You may find more than one CKR spinning at a time. Allow them to continue to spin as long as the recipient requires.

With your understanding that these fields can help the recipient shift into a higher level of awareness while releasing energy, beliefs and memories at lower levels, you can set the intention for the symbols to continue to spin until the healing that the recipient is ready for at this time is completed.

You can close the session as you normally would. You will want to briefly explain to your recipient that they may feel shifts in their beliefs and awareness and to be open to the changes. Remind them that their body is choosing what beliefs to release for their highest good.

You can also ask them to take some time the following week to be quiet and meditate for 10-15 minutes each day or to just focus on their breath.

You may want to practice using this technique on yourself initially to get a sense of how using the 3D CKR feels. Then when you feel ready and called to, you can work with others. As your awareness deepens, so will your understanding of how perception impacts reality. This awareness will help you to work with clients at a deeper level.

I have found this technique to be very powerful and positive in my practice. I hope you find this to be a meaningful tool as well.

Using Reiki in Spaces

Just as people vibrate at a specific frequency which can be influenced by the emotions/memories/beliefs that are being stored, a room, home, building or land can also hold a vibration. As a Reiki practitioner, you have the ability to perform a Reiki session on a space just as you would a human.

First you will want to make sure you are working not only with the space, but also with the inhabitants of the space. The inhabitants can impact their surroundings and vice versa. Usually when there is a strong dissonant energy in a house for example, the potential home buyers will not choose the house as "it just feels wrong" to them. In the cases where the space has shifted in frequency, sometimes when individuals go through times of extreme stress, their energy is lowered and they can impact the space around them with that energy being absorbed.

The other reason you will want to work with the inhabitants associated with the space is that when there is such a strong dissonance between the inhabitants and any energy seeking a home to reside in, those high energy individuals are not attractive for lower frequencies and will be less affected by any lower frequencies around them. You may find performing a session on the inhabitant as a surrogate for the space helpful. Their head for example may represent the highest level of the space and their feet the basement or lowest level. With this method, Reiki will be addressing any imbalances that connect the inhabitant and the space.

Once the inhabitants are receiving Reiki, you can go into the space and do an intake just as you would with your clients. What are the imbalances you are sensing? Are they located in specific areas? What other information are you receiving as you explore the space. You may find going into your mental Reiki room helpful in accessing information. Keeping a detailed progress chart will help you to measure progress.

After the intake, open the windows where possible and allow each room to draw Reiki energy in. Observe the rooms as they are filled and beaming Reiki energy. You can use the Reiki symbols when called to. The traditional CKR can help to release negative energy, the SHK to release emotional/mental energy and the HSZSN to go back in time to release energy as well as into the future to help infuse Reiki energy. The DKM can be used to help the inhabitants work through their deep, life lessons more smoothly.

Some practitioners like to also use sound (a chime/singing bowl etc.) and fire (candle or smudge stick) but that is up to you.

When working with spaces, try to release the agenda that you want the energy to move or shift as that can limit the work. Also, let go of any judgements around energy being negative or positive and see it as different frequencies. Just observe and allow the space the drawn in Reiki energy :). Once you have completed the session, be wary of the information you pass on to your client. I have had countless clients come to me with stories that they have attached to which makes clearing the energy much more difficult. By keeping your discussions simple, the client's egoic mind is not concerned with the story behind the energy and instead moves forward with the new frequencies around them.

Reiju Meditation for Self

It is said that with his teachings, Dr Usui performed what is known as Reiju empowerments with his students before he began the practice of attunements. Reiju can be translated as "to confer/receive spirit." These empowerments were different than attunements in that the student would be able to draw in energy in that space and during that time to deepen their awareness. This meditation was a shared experience between Master and student and is thought to have origins in Tendai Buddhism. Usui did not perform any specific movements during this process but over time his students created a physical ritual that could be completed. Here is a sample of a ritual you could perform with yourself if it resonates.

1. Take a few deep breaths and clear your mind.
2. Visualize your heart center opening.
3. Raise your hands above your head in line with your shoulders with your palms facing up and your fingers pointing outward.
4. Observe Reiki energy coming down through your crown chakra and hands all the way down to your navel or sacral chakra.
5. Rest your hands on your abdomen.
6. Feel the connection to Reiki energy.
7. Raise your hands above your head and allow Reiki energy to fill your body until you are beaming with it.
8. Then place your hands on your abdomen again.

9. You can repeat this process again until you feel it is time to close the meditation.

Performing Reiju with Others

You will have the recipient sitting on a chair with their hands in prayer/Gassho position.

You will begin with your hands also in Gassho position and clear and center your mind. You may find visualizing the DKM symbol helpful.

Touch the recipient's shoulder to let them know you will begin.

Raise your hands above your head with your palms facing up and your fingers pointing outwards and allow Reiki energy to flow through them.

Move your hands in a continuous motion down and in front of the recipient's body visualizing the Reiki energy coming down through them and clearing their body from their crown chakra down. Observe each energy center opening as Reiki flows through. Your hands will travel down past the recipient's knees until they have almost reached the floor. If you choose you can move onto specific areas or you can ground the energy through the floor first. See what feels right.

Now you will be holding positions as you allow Reiki energy to fill various centers in the recipient's body. You will observe the energy flow and the centers clear and open. You will want to hold each position for a minimum of ten seconds.

Sahasrara chakra (crown):

- You will stand up and place your hands one on top of the other, about three to five inches above the student's head.
- Watch Reiki energy flow down and along the spine.
- Observe the crown chakra as it is filled with energy.

Temples:
- Slowly move your hands to the sides of the student's head so that your palms are facing towards the temples.
- Observe the area filling with Reiki energy.

Ajna chakra: (Third Eye):
- Move your hands in front of the student's face and form a triangle with your index fingers and thumbs. Your palms are facing the student and the triangle window will be in front of the third eye chakra. 
- Observe Reiki energy flow into the third eye chakra.

Vishudda chakra: (Throat):
- Move your hands down to the throat with one hand in front and the other behind, watching Reiki energy flood the throat chakra.

Anahata chakra (Heart):
- Move your hands behind and in front of, the heart area, and allow pure Reiki energy to flow to the heart chakra.

Hands:
- Bringing your fingertips together, move them down and around the recipient's hands, without touching their hands.
- Allow Reiki energy to flow through their hands, up through their arms and shoulders.
- Bring your hands down the recipient's body and ground the energy by touching the floor.

Conclusion:
- You will close Reiju by placing your hands in Gassho position and giving thanks.

Distance Reiju

Just as Reiki sessions and attunements can be effectively performed from a distance, Reiju can also transcend time and space.

To perform a distance Reiju, you can enter your mental Reiki room and invite the recipient in. You will then perform the Reiju as you would in person through your mind's eye.

Living Reiki

Now that you are practicing daily self-treatments and perhaps working with others, you can take Reiki to the next level by bringing it into your life each day.

A Reiki Master is one who is able to apply the Reiki principles to all aspects of their life. Just as you are the observer in your Reiki sessions, trusting that the energy will flow where needed, you will also be present and observe the unfolding of your life, trusting that the universal life force energy will guide you.

In a Reiki session, you do not diagnose or prescribe and in your life you will strive not to judge or react. Rather you will focus on being in the moment and responding to events and individuals as your intuition and heart guide you.

With Reiki, we work to help ourselves and others release energy, beliefs and memories that block energy flow and prevent us from seeing the perfection in ourselves and those around us. This is usually not an instantaneous release and can take time as your body slowly releases that which is not serving your highest self.

In the meantime, you will find you are triggered. Emotions may rise up, you may feel suffering and conflict. Resistance will only make it worse, so try to breathe and observe the energy. Being aware of the energy will help it to transmute. You may be tempted to project it onto others or push it down within. Instead - surrender and see that this this is an opportunity for profound healing if you are open to seeing things in a new light.

Thoughts will usually present themselves to you. Your brain is like a calculator. Let your brain do the job it was intended to do such as help you with everyday tasks. When your thoughts are fueled by the dissonant energy within, you will find emotions attached to your thoughts. Any time you are feeling stressed, this is a warning from your bodymind to let you know that your thoughts are not serving your highest self.

As we grow up we are taught to discern one thing from another. That is white, this is tall, that is hot. This helps us to survive. As adults, our inner evolution depends on us moving past the labels and judgements so we can see the connections and bigger picture. Just as in our Reiki sessions, we do not focus on a single organ or body part, in our lives we need to find balance by looking at our lives as a whole. When we are able to release our judgement of ourselves and others, our perception is strengthened and clear.

As we release blocks to the energy flow within, our perception of energy in and around us will also likely be refined. This can be a wonderful way to access information and can add a richness to your life.

Commonly known as empathic abilities, you may find you are more able to sense the energy in others and environments. This is our natural state of being. Some people find the desire to protect themselves from this energy. This fear does not serve their spiritual awakening as it constricts their energy and usually adds to the beliefs and energy that they are working so diligently to clear with Reiki energy. In that fearful place of needing protection, a person's natural energetic resonance is lowered making them more attractive for lower frequencies. In essence, the fear and need for protection attracts negativity.

Rather than constricting in fear when confronted with dissonant energy, we need to expand and resonate with high frequency energy. You can do so by drawing in Reiki energy and beaming it like a lantern. Energetically, you become the light.

When you are in large groups or with individuals you do not resonate with, focus on your breath and drawing in Reiki energy. When you feel it beaming from you, observe your environment. You will likely find that things look and feel quite differently. You may also become aware of how your own energy is contributing to the collective energy around you.

When faced with decisions in your life, using Reiki can help you to access information that would be helpful for you. For example, when considering a career move or a change in your relationship you could begin a self-treatment in your mental Reiki room and imagine viewing a screen in your room with your current state. You then fast forward 5 years with the new job or change in relationship. Continuing your self-treatment, how are you feeling? In many cases when faced with a decision, we react based on the thoughts we have. Remembering that our thoughts can be fueled by dissonant energy within makes them not as reliable as using information gleaned from our highest self.

Just as we are present in our Reiki sessions, with a clear mind free of judgement we can also hold that awareness in our daily lives. In our Reiki sessions, we are active in that we perform the positions as we feel called to but we release any expectations around what the outcome should be. The same can be said in our lives. We can play and explore without expecting things to occur in a certain way. The same wisdom that guides energy within our bodies is the same energy that guides our lives. Just as Reiki works through us as practitioners, let your life live through you.

You are powerful - it is time you truly embrace your potential.

Congratulations on completing the Master Level! You will decide where your journey with Reiki will take you.

About the Author

Lisa Powers is a Reiki Master/Teacher and has had the honor of sharing the gift of Reiki for the past fifteen years. To date, Lisa has taught Reiki and self-development courses to over 35,000 students and continues to create and teach courses that serve as tools for healing and enlightenment. Lisa loves to learn about advances in alternative health and science. In her spare time, you can find Lisa sitting in quiet contemplation by water with her dog on her lap.

Courses currently taught by Lisa Powers

Reiki Level I, II Master Certification

Animal Reiki Certification

Reiki Business Course

Crystal Reiki Certification

Essential Oils for Wellness

Please visit https://onlinereikicourse.com for additional resources, course information and updates.

Printed in Great Britain
by Amazon